Blind Men
and
Elephants

Blind Men
and
Elephants

Perspectives on Humor

Arthur Asa Berger

Transaction Publishers
New Brunswick (U.S.A.) and London (U.K.)

Library of Congress Catalog Number: 94-27138
ISBN: 1-56000-185-2
Printed in the United States of America

Library of Congress Cataloging-in-Publication Data

Berger, Arthur Asa, 1933–
    Blind men and elephants : perspectives on humor / Arthur Asa Berger.
        p. cm.
    Includes bibliographical references and index.
    ISBN 1-56000-185-2
    1. Wit and humor—History and criticism. I. Title.
PN6147.B48   1995
801'.957—dc20   94-27138
                                                                          CIP

Contents

Acknowledgments

I owe an enormous debt of gratitude to the many writers and researchers from a variety of disciplines and fields of knowledge who have written about humor, comedy, irony, wit, and related concerns and who have provided me with ideas and insights that I have used in this book. I have benefitted from the works (and in some cases the acquaintance or friendship) of William Fry, Harvey Mindess, Aaron Wildavsky, Tom Inge, Mary Douglas, Avner Ziv, Daniel Dayan, Elihu Katz (I call the two of them Danielihu), Marshall McLuhan, George Gerbner, Irving Louis Horowitz, Mitch Allen, Victor Raskin, Stan Lee, Umberto Eco, Martin Grotjahn, Vladimir Propp, Christie Davies, M.M. Bakhtin, Ferdinand de Saussure, Henri Bergson, Sigmund Freud, Aristotle, and many others. I've also gained a great deal from the wonderful writers, cartoonists, comic-strip artists, stand-up comedians, playwrights, and movie makers who have provided material for me and other students of humor to work with. I owe a particular debt of gratitude to my colleagues in the Broadcast & Electronic Communication Arts Department at San Francisco State University, who have been extremely supportive of my work, and to my students, who have good naturedly tolerated my puns and other attempts at comedy and who have, from time to time, provided me with some very fine and useful jokes.

A joke is a play on form. It brings into relation disparate elements in such a way that one accepted pattern is challenged by the appearance of another which in some way was hidden in the first. I confess that I find Freud's definition of the joke highly satisfactory. The joke is an image of the relaxation of conscious control in favour of the subconscious.

—Mary Douglas
"Jokes"

Preface

Writing one book on humor can be looked upon, by those who have a charitable disposition, as a youthful (or, in my case, not so youthful) indiscretion. But what does one make of someone who writes two books on humor? In an earlier book, *An Anatomy of Humor,* I dealt with a typology I'd developed—some forty-five techniques that, I suggested, are at the heart of humor. I explained the techniques and then applied them to a variety of examples—everything from jokes to *Twelfth Night* to *Huckleberry Finn* and Jewish humor.

In this book I do something else. I provide a number of what might be called "case histories" that deal with the way scholars from a variety of different disciplines and scholarly domains try to make sense of humor. I've also used jokes and humorous texts not found in my first book, though I must confess there are, perhaps, a couple of jokes that I borrowed from *An Anatomy of Humor* in this book. Finding good jokes that can be used for scholarly concerns is not the easiest thing to do, believe me.

One of the chapters in this book is co-authored. I started writing an article on humor with Aaron Wildavsky using his work on political cultures and had roughed in the article when he suddenly took sick and, after only a few months, died of lung cancer. Before he became ill I sent him a draft and he made a considerable number of comments and suggestions; he also supplied some jokes. We spent some time talking about the article on the phone, as well. So the article represents, to some extent, a collaboration. But he never saw the final draft. We had talked, from time to time, of writing a book together on humor and this article was, in a sense, a start on that project.

Some scholarly work on humor makes a point of not being funny; there are, after all, scholars who use humor as some kind of a variable but are really interested in other things. This book doesn't follow that pattern; I've included a large number of jokes (because they are short and relatively easy to deal with) and other humorous texts. An unfunny book on humor strikes me as somewhat of an oxymoron.

Since this book has elephants in the title, let me conclude with an elephant joke—or, more precisely, an elephant riddle:

What did the elephant say to the naked man?

How do you get enough to eat with that?

If you found that riddle amusing and are curious about why it amused you, and want to know "what's so funny about that?"—read on.

Because of the all-pervading scope and extremely diverse nature of humor, it can be studied by scholars from many disciplines, from the humanities to the natural sciences. The history of humor research demonstrates that such indeed has been the case; philosophers, literary critics, literary biographers and historians, sociologists, folklorists, psychologists, physicians, and scholars from various other disciplines have studied humor since antiquity.

Humor scholars are like blind men who need to view their work within the total context of the field of humorology while simultaneously describing and discussing with their colleagues in the field what they discover in order to come to some consensus as to what this elephant of humor is like. They could also learn to look at the subject from disciplinary perspectives other than their own.

—M.L. Apte
"Disciplinary Boundaries
in Humorology: An
Anthropologist's Ruminations"

1

Mirrors on Mirth: Making Sense of Humor

This book is about the different ways people from a variety of fields and disciplines try to make sense of humor. *Blind Men and Elephants* is not meant to be a humorous book, per se, though it does have a good deal of humor in it and I believe you will find it, in many places, amusing and entertaining. I think humorless books about humor are a bad idea; some would say, of course, that all books about humor are a bad idea.

But humor is too important a subject to be ignored and has become, in recent years, a subject of great interest in academic circles and elsewhere. There is an international academic journal, *Humor*, devoted to the subject; there are yearly conferences on humor sponsored by the International Society for Humor Studies; other organizations, all over the world, hold conferences on humor; and there are even several book clubs devoted solely to books on humor.

Nevertheless, humor continues to confound us. We've never figured out how to deal with it. Thus, in an influential book, *Humour and Laughter: Theory, Research and Applications,* editors Tony Chapman and Hugh Foot (1976,4) write:

> No all embracing theory of humour and/or laughter has yet gained widespread acceptance and possibly no general theory will ever be successfully applied to the human race as a whole when its members exhibit such vast individual differences with respect to their humour responsiveness. The paradox associated with humour is almost certainly a function of its being incorrectly viewed as a unitary process. Humor plays a myriad of roles and serves a number of quite different functions.

It is this complexity that Chapman and Foot mention that led me to adopt the approach I have taken, using a variety of different case histories to shed different perspectives on humor.

A complex phenomenon like humor demands, I would suggest, a multidisciplinary approach, and that is the methodology I have used.

3

The case histories reflect the positions of scholars from a number of different areas and disciplines, but the scholarly positions taken reflect only one of many possible approaches that could be taken within a given discipline, since disciplines (as well as multidisciplinary departments) are not unitary and are not made up of likeminded people.

The Problem of Reading Humorous Texts

Let me return to Chapman and Foot's comment about the variety of responses members of the human race give to humor. This matter of human variability is at the heart of the reader-response school of literary theory.

The development of reader-response theory raises an interesting question about humor. If everyone "reads" (sees, interprets, makes sense of) literary works, films, television shows, and so forth his or her own way, so to speak, why is it that audiences tend to respond with laughter, more or less at the same time, to jokes told by stand-up comedians or humorous parts of films?

Wolfgang Iser, one of the leading reader-response or reception theorists, argues that one can make a distinction between a literary work (and in the case of humor we can add a subliterary work, such as a joke, comic strip, animated film, cartoon, etc.) and the experience a reader has in reading the work. As he writes in his essay "The Reading Process: A Phenomenological Approach" (Lodge, 1988, 212):

> The texts as such offer different "schematized views" through which the subject matter of the work can come to light, but the actual bringing to light is an action of *Konkretisation*. If this is so, then the literary work has two poles, which we might call the artistic and the aesthetic: the artistic refers to the text created by the author, and the aesthetic to the realization accomplished by the reader. From this polarity it follows that the literary work cannot be completely identical with the text, or with the realization of the text, but in fact must lie halfway between the two. The work is more than the text, for the text only takes on life when it is realized, and furthermore the realization is by no means independent of the individual disposition of the reader.

We have, then, with literary texts (and other kinds of texts as well) two poles: the artistic and the aesthetic. The artistic is created by the author and the aesthetic is realized by the reader. When readers read a text, they bring what Iser calls a "literary work" into existence, and it is neither the text nor the reading, but something, a state that Iser calls "virtuality," in between.

From this point of view, the intentions of the author of a text are not of the utmost significance, for different readers, based on their individual dispositions, get different things out of a given text. The author creates the text but it is nothing without a reader and the reader, by reading, helps bring into being the literary work. As Iser puts it, "The phenomenological theory of art lays full stress on the idea that, in considering a literary work, one must take into account not only the actual text but also, and in equal measure, the actions involved in responding to that text" (Lodge, 1988, 212). The old idea of privileging the text and assuming that all readers will have the same responses and get the same ideas (very similar to the hypodermic needle theory of communication) is rejected.

People differ greatly in terms of their education, socioeconomic level, race, religion, ethnicity, gender, sexual orientation, politics, and so on. Is it any surprise that given these differences (and the passions that they seem to engender in individuals nowadays) that we should suggest that readers get different things out of what they read and interpret the texts they read in a variety of ways?

I would like to suggest that we use the term *reading* broadly, and use it to deal with our experiences with all kinds of works—not only literary ones (by which is meant "elite" works of literature) but nonliterary, or what we used to describe as subliterary, ones. For our purposes, when we talk about texts, we will not limit ourselves to the great works of literary humor by Shakespeare, Molière, Gogol, or Mark Twain, but also include, in our understanding of what texts are, jokes, comic strips, cartoons, graffiti, sitcoms, comic plays and films, and so on.

Let us return now to the problem (mentioned earlier) that arises with humorous texts, such as jokes and humorous films: at some times audiences, made up of readers, listeners, or viewers who all read texts differently, so the reader-response theorists tell us, often respond, at the same time, with laughter. How might one explain this?

One answer is that humorous texts are what Umberto Eco calls "open texts." He distinguishes between "closed texts," which are open, more or less, to any interpretation, and "open texts," which allegedly have the capacity to force readers to use texts in prescribed ways. Eco points out in his introduction to *The Role of the Reader* (1984, 8) that people come from a variety of different backgrounds, which affects the way they decode (make sense of) texts:

> In the process of communication, a text is frequently interpreted against the background of codes different from those intended by the author. Some authors do not take into account such a possibility. They have in mind an average addressee referred to a given social context. Nobody can say what happens when the actual reader is different from the "average" one.

Eco (1984, 8) then distinguishes between two kinds of texts—open and closed ones—and writes:

> Those texts that obsessively aim at arousing a precise response on the part of to more or less precise empirical readers (be they children, soap-opera addicts, doctors, law-abiding citizens, swingers, Presbyterians, farmers, middle-class women, scuba divers, effete snobs, or any other imaginable sociopsychological category) are in fact open to any possible aberrant decoding. A text so immoderately 'open' to every possible interpretation will be called a *closed* one.

He suggests that Superman comic strips and Ian Fleming's novels about James Bond belong to this category.

Eco then describes another kind of text, *open* texts, which, he suggests, is quite different from closed ones. *Open* texts don't allow readers to decode the texts any way they want to. As Eco (1984, 9) writes: "You cannot use the text as you want, but only as the text wants you to use it. An open text, however 'open' it be, cannot afford whatever interpretation." If Eco is correct, and there are texts that are actually *open,* humorous texts might be good examples of this category. After all, these texts try to create the kind of model readers they want—people who will respond with smiles, laughter, and related feelings to a text.

But the notion of open readers also suggests that reader-response theorists oversimplify things and do not recognize that in certain situations, readers do not have any latitude, so to speak, about how they will make sense of a text. There is another possibility that would fit within reader-response theory, namely, that although different readers get many different things out of a text, based on their backgrounds, there are, nevertheless, certain commonalities in what they get, generated by the text, that, in the case of humorous works, enable them to respond by laughter, as long as the subject of the joke or humor does not deal with matters and subjects about which the various individuals have very strong beliefs and feelings.

There is also, of course, the matter of arousal and contagion and it may be that a few people (the equivalent of humor opinion leaders) laughing in an audience will induce many others to laugh, even though they may not think they've seen or heard anything terribly funny. People go to see stand-up comics and comedies (films and plays) because they want to laugh and be amused, so they are predisposed to find things humorous.

We might keep this matter of why people who allegedly interpret works differently laugh at the same time in the back of our heads as we pursue our investigation of how different disciplines, metadisciplines, and methodologies make sense of humor. Although it is not generally thought of as pertaining to the question of reader-response or reception theory, John Godfrey Saxe's poem about some blind men from Hindustan and an elephant is relevant and can be thought of as a good example of what reception theorists have in mind when they talk about how different people make sense of a given work.

The Blind Men of Hindustan and the Rashomon Phenomenon

Let me quote John Godfrey Saxe's famous poem "The Blind Men and the Elephant." This poem shows that people see (or in this case experience) things in different ways—elephants and, as I have suggested, jokes and other forms of humor—a matter that is also at the heart of Kurosawa's marvelous film *Rashomon*.

THE BLIND MEN AND THE ELEPHANT

It was six men of Indostan
To learning much inclined.
Who went to see the Elephant
(Tho' all of them were blind)
That each by observation
Might satisfy his mind.

The first approached the elephant
And happening to fall
Against his broad and sturdy side
At once began to bawl:
"God bless me! But the elephant
Is very like a wall."

The second feeling of the tusk,
Cried "How, what have we here
So very round and smooth and sharp?
to me 'tis mighty clear
This wonder of an elephant
Is very like a spear."

The third approached the animal
And happening to take
The squirming trunk within his hands
Thus boldly up and spake:
"I see," quoth he, "the Elephant
Is very like a snake."

The fourth reached out an eager hand
and felt about the knee.
"What most of this wondrous beast is like
Is might plain," quoth he.
"T'is clear enough the elephant
Is very like a tree."

The fifth chanced to touch the ear
Said "E'en the blindest man
can tell what this resembles most;
Deny the fact who can
This marvel of an elephant
Is very like a fan."

The sixth no sooner had begun
About the beast to grope
That seizing on the swinging tail
That fell within his scope
"I see," quoth he, "the elephant
Is very like a rope."

And so these men of Indostan
Disputed loud and long,
Each in his own opinion
Exceeding stiff and strong,
Though each was partly in the right,
And all were in the wrong.

The Rashomon Phenomenon

What we have here is a phenomenon sometimes known as the *Rashomon* phenomenon, after the brilliant film that shows a bandit having sex with a woman in front of her husband (who is tied up and helpless) and who, later on, is found dead. The film then offers completely different perspectives on what happened from the points of view of four "readers": the bandit, the dead husband (who communicates via a psychic), the wife, and a wood gatherer who accidentally stumbled upon the scene and observed things.

Although *Rashomon* is not considered a comedy, to the extent that it offers four different explanations of an event and exposes people as liars, cheats, and cowards, it has a comic dimension to it. It poses a problem for us: What really happened? What can we know? Thus, it does have a comic as well as a cosmic dimension to it.

The four different explanations can be seen, by stretching things, perhaps, as equivalent to four "punch lines" that are told after the first part of the story—the rape/seduction involving the bandit and the woman. This story is based on the variations on a theme technique, which is used in many jokes and humorous stories. These stories generally deal with how members of different nationalities or occupations deal with something:

> *There is a shipwreck and two men end up on a desert island with a woman. If the two men are French, one marries the woman and the other becomes her lover. If they are English, nothing happens because they haven't been introduced. If they are Russian, they send a note to Moscow in a bottle asking for instructions.*

A Multidisciplinary Perspective

In this book, what I have done is substituted scholars, each of whom comes from a particular discipline, metadiscipline, or mode of analysis, for "the blind men of learning" of Indostan. Let me point out that these case histories that I am offering are those that a scholar with a particular disciplinary perspective is offering, and this disciplinary perspective is not to be construed as the only method or approach found in the discipline being dealt with. (It might be argued that some scholars in any given discipline tend to be, like the men of Indostan, "blind" to perspectives, points of view, and paradigms not in their school or approach.)

Each of the case histories, then, sheds light on some facet or aspect of humor and this combination of approaches will be, I would suggest, of considerable value. For the elephant I've substituted humor, a "beast" infinitely more complicated to deal with than elephants, though we now recognize that elephant behavior is much more complex than we have previously imagined.

Like the men of Indostan, also, my scholars will be partially right in that their analyses will offer insights about humor that will be valuable and useful, but not complete. I agree with Chapman and Foot about humor; I don't think there is a single way, a "royal road" to deal with humor, in all its complexity and variety, but we can shed light on it from different perspectives and illuminate as much of it as possible.

This multidisciplinary approach is discussed in John Brewer and Albert Hunter's book *Multimethod Research: A Synthesis of Styles* (1989, 16–17). They write:

> [S]ocial science methods should not be treated as mutually exclusive alternatives among which we must choose and then passively pay the costs of our choices. Our individual methods may be flawed but the flaws in each are not identical. A diversity of imperfection allows us to combine methods not only to gain their individual strengths but so to compensate for the particular faults and limitations. The multimethod approach is largely built on this insight. Its fundamental strategy is to *attack a research problem with an arsenal of methods that have nonoverlapping weaknesses in addition to their complementary strengths.*

By using a number of approaches, each of which is reflected in a case history that adds interesting and useful insights, we can make some progress in dealing with this most difficult subject, humor.

I've used the following approaches, techniques, disciplines, meta-disciplines, areas (what you will) in this book: literary theory, rhetorical theory, semiotics, communication theory, sociology, psychology, philosophy, political science, and visual aesthetics. These perspectives are not, I realize, in all cases mutually exclusive (communication, for example, involves many different areas), but they do represent some of the more important domains used to understand humor and its relation to individuals and groups in society.

I chose these disciplines and perspectives because they tend to be the ones most commonly found in the scholarly literature about humor and, I believe, are the most useful ones in dealing with humor. Everyone, more or less, has something to say about humor—but some perspectives are more useful than others and lead to more interesting insights.

Humor, Comedy, Jokes, Laughter: A Note on Terminology

Curiously enough, it is very difficult to define humor. It is connected, generally, with laughter (a physical response involving certain physiological activities), with mirth, with gaiety, with feeling good, and that kind of thing. Comedy, technically speaking, refers to literary works that use humor to achieve their ends. Some works are completely comic while others, tragicomedies, have elements of comedy in them.

A joke, as I will use the term (and this is the conventional definition of a joke), is a relatively short narrative, meant to amuse and be funny, that contains a punch line. Thus, a joke is a very particular form of humor and, what needs to be emphasized, jokes are not to be equated with humor. I will deal with jokes in more detail shortly. In this book I will make use of a number of jokes, because they are short and thus easy to reproduce and relatively easy to deal with.

Eight Scholars Analyze a Joke

As a preview of what you will find in this book, I will present a joke and then offer eight different interpretations of the joke, each one based on a particular discipline or perspective. I should point out here that jokes are often insulting and frequently contain a great deal of hostility. The same applies to humor of all kinds. A considerable amount of ridicule is found directed toward women, men, dogs, cats, psychiatrists, politicians, professors, African-Americans, Jews, Catholics, Protestants, Muslims, the clergy, gay people, straight people, you name it. I repeat this humor not because I wish to insult any group but because I wish to show relevant examples. If I had to limit myself to humor that didn't insult anyone I'd have very little material that I could use. So let me apologize for printing this material and assure my readers that I do not wish to offend anyone.

THE GAY MAN AND THE BAR

A man walks into a bar. "I'm Jim," he says to the bartender. "I'm gay. Will you serve me?" "Sure," says the bartender. "What will you have?" "A beer," says Jim. The next day Jim walks into the bar, with another man. "This is my brother Bob," he says to the bartender. "He's gay. Will you serve us?" "Of course," says the bartender. "What'll you guys have?" "Two beers," says Jim. The next day Jim and Bob walk into the bar accompanied by another man. "This is my brother Sam," says Jim. "He's gay. Will you serve us?" "Yes," says the bartender. "What do you guys want?" "Three beers" says Jim. After the bartender serves the men the beers he asks "Does anyone in your family like women?" "Of course," says Jim. "Our sister Sally does, but she doesn't drink."

Let's see, now, how each of our scholars would analyze this joke. These analyses will be brief and are only meant to suggest the kinds of things people with different perspectives concern themselves with when dealing with a joke or any text (the term conventionally used in literary studies for any work, such as a story, novel, poem, television program, and so on). I will offer more extended discussions of the various perspectives in the book.

The Rhetorical Approach

For our purposes, the rhetorician will focus on the techniques used to generate the humor in this text. The most important technique, I would suggest, is one I call "Disappointment and Defeated Expectations." The punch line in this joke, "Of course," suggests that at least one member of the family is heterosexual, but it turns out not to be the case, for the member of the family that likes women is a woman, and thus the family remains firmly homosexual. In this respect, it is most unusual and thus we find the techniques of eccentricity, comic types, and that kind of thing at work, also. In addition, there is the repetition, in which we are introduced to the first, second, and third brother, thus heightening the significance of the question by the bartender ("Does anyone...like women?") and of the punch line ("Of course...our sister Sally does...").

Semiotic Analysis

One of the important techniques semioticians use when they deal with texts is to consider their paradigmatic structure—the set of oppositions found in them (some would say read into them) that give them meaning. Concepts have meaning, Saussure argued, due to their relationships with other concepts in their system; nothing has meaning in itself. Thus, a paradigmatic analysis of this joke would yield the following set of hidden oppositions:

NORMAL	DEVIANT
Heterosexuality	Homosexuality
Bartender	Brothers and Sister
Males like Women	Females like Women

The joke is based on this set of linked notions that are found under each main concept. Listeners to the joke don't necessarily bring this set of oppositions to mind, but they must recognize it if the joke is to make any sense and the punch line is to be effective. When the bartender asks whether anyone in the family likes women, the question assumes the polarity between normal and deviant (we cannot use negations in making our oppositions because they don't tell us enough). The bartender assumed he was asking about males in the family who liked women, about people who were "normal." The punch line only makes sense in that context, and its humor comes from the way it defeats our expectation of normalcy.

Communication Theory

Communication theory is a very broad field. In this book I deal with Roman Jakobson's model, which involves an addresser, an addressee, coding and decoding of a message, and so forth. I point out that according to some communication theorists, a message has information to the extent that it has a surprise. Thus, all jokes, since they have punch lines, contain information. In this joke, the information conveyed by the punch line is that the sister of the gay brothers is a lesbian and thus, everyone in the family is gay.

I also deal with the matter of aberrant decoding, a situation in which a person does not interpret a message the way the sender wants the message to be interpreted. For a joke to work, the addressee must understand the message and have the same assumptions the sender has. Thus, when the bartender asks, "Does anyone in your family like women?" the addressee must interpret that question correctly and assume, correctly, that the bartender is talking about heterosexual relationships. That is what sets up the punch line, "Of course. Our sister Sally does...but she doesn't drink." That's why she hasn't come to the bar.

Psychoanalytic Perspectives

From the psychological and psychoanalytic perspective, it is the sexuality of the members of the family that is of paramount importance. The heroes of this little story are gay men, all of whom are members of the same family. The psychoanalytic perspective on homosexuality, as explained in Hinsie and Campbell's *Psychiatric Dictionary* (fourth edition) is as follows:

> Freud pointed out that fear of castration, intense Oedipal attachment to the mother, narcissism and narcissistic object choice, and identification with sibling rivals with secondary overcompensatory love for them are important etiological factors in male homosexuality. (1970, 350)

The authors point out that some believe this behavior is genetically determined, though most researchers do not.

In any case, this joke would suggest that at the heart of the family is a very strong mother who has been, the theory outlined above suggests, the major factor in shaping the behavior of the sons. What this joke does, however, is place homosexuality in a different light, as something relatively normal. It plays with the listener, who is tricked by the punch line. The bartender has really asked, in a roundabout way, isn't anyone in your family normal? What's normal in one family is not normal in another. Seen this way, the joke is liberating and frees us from being bound by conventional ideas and beliefs.

This notion that humor can be "liberating" is a very important one, for it suggests that humor has intrinsic therapeutic value, which may explain why so many people feel the need to experience humor on a daily basis.

Sociological Analysis

In my chapter I focus on functionalism and related concerns: phenomena that are dysfunctional, that are nonfunctional, that have manifest functions, that have latent functions, the matter of functional alternatives, and so on. (This is only one small aspect of sociological thought, of course, but it is useful for our purposes.)

What are the functions of this joke for the teller and the listener? First, telling the joke helps build a sense of togetherness, helps integrate the teller and the listener into a group (those listening to the joke). The manifest function of telling the joke is to amuse others, to be looked upon favorably as someone who has a sense of humor, who is amusing and entertaining. We can say this about joke telling in general. But the latent function of the joke is to establish more strongly, to firm up the teller's (and listener's) heterosexual identity, to demonstrate that one is "normal" by laughing at those who are supposedly not normal, who are deviant. But the joke is not really a hostile one; it is amusing and tricks the listener, whose assumptions are shown to be false. So the joke demonstrates that one is not a hater of gay people but, instead, one who might be seen as somewhat sympathetic to them.

Finally, telling this joke can be seen as a functional alternative to hostile and perhaps even violent behavior. Humor is a means of dealing with aggressive tendencies a person might have verbally rather than physically and telling jokes is a way of dealing with hostility in an acceptable, relatively speaking, manner.

Philosophical Approaches

Philosophers, as I point out in my chapter on philosophical approaches to humor, have generally concerned themselves with the nature of humor in general, its ontological status, and that kind of thing. Aristotle argued that we laugh at people we see as ridiculous, as inferior to ourselves. He is one of the fathers of the "superiority" theory of humor. From this perspective, the humor in the joke comes from our being able to feel superior to the gay brothers and their lesbian sister.

Bergson argued that humor involves "the mechanical encrusted on the living" and suggested that this manifests itself in many ways, one of which was comic types. By this he meant people who are fixated, rigid, inflexible, such as misers, misanthropes, and so forth. Wherever you have a type, he wrote, you have humor. The gay brothers in this joke represent comic types; there's something mechanical and rigid here (all members of the family are gay) where there should be flexibility and variety. The question the bartender asks, as a matter of fact, is based on this notion of flexibility and variety. But the punch line shows that the family is all gay, thus defeating our expectations of normalcy, flexibility, and so on.

Political Science

In my chapter on politics and humor, I have a section dealing with political cultures and the work of Aaron Wildavsky. He has suggested, in a number of essays and books, that there are four political cultures found in democratic societies (he actually has revised things and added a fifth one, but it is small and not significant for our purposes). These cultures are formed due to the nature of the prescriptions groups place on members of groups and the boundaries that exist among groups. We end up with four political cultures: egalitarians, (hierarchical) elitists, (competitive) individualists, and fatalists. People sometimes change political cultures and are not locked into a given group for life, though fatalists generally find it difficult to escape from that position.

I argue, pushing things to extremes perhaps, that a given joke, based on the values it supports or attacks, should appeal primarily to one of these political cultures (or people moving toward a given political culture), since it reinforces their beliefs. Conversely, it should not appeal to the other groups since it attacks their values.

In this context, the joke would be seen as essentially an egalitarian one, since it presents homosexuality in a relatively benign manner. The joke, we might say, "normalizes" homosexuality and, by doing so, appeals to egalitarian values, which stress the things that unite people rather than those that divide them, and the equality of needs we all have. An elitist joke would have made gays objects of ridicule and suggested that gays are inferior to heterosexuals. A fatalist joke would have suggested that being gay was a matter of bad luck or something like that, and that there was nothing for gays to do except resign themselves to their fate, to persecution, and that kind of thing. And a competitive individualist joke might involve something such as seeing who could bash gays more.

We might also remember that humor can be used to control people (especially in small groups) or to resist control. The joke might be seen as a means of resisting control. The gays, who are the heroes of the joke, show a bit of anxiety about their marginal status ("We're gay. Will you serve us?") but also feel at ease, since each member of the family is gay. Gay-bashing jokes are attempts to stigmatize homosexuals and isolate them and, in doing so, control them. Jokes that treat gays as relatively ordinary members of society, as no more eccentric or weird than others, have the opposite effect and are a form of resistance.

A Feminist Perspective

Finally, let me offer what I think would be a feminist perspective. The joke assumes a phallocentric world—one in which normalcy involves men liking women. Remember that the punch line is based on a question the bartender asks the brothers. "Does anyone in your family like women?" This question, as I've indicated earlier, assumes a heterosexual orientation in contrast to the three brothers, each of whom is gay. When the bartender asked this question, he thought he was asking whether there were any males in the family who were heterosexual. Asking this question privileges the phallus and, in addition, focuses attention on male sexuality. It indicates the existence of a patriarchal society in which women are of secondary importance in the scheme of things. This is the case even though all the children in the family (that we are told about) are homosexuals.

We might note, also, that Sally, the sister, is only mentioned; she is not actually brought into the bar, like each of the three brothers. Thus, she ends up playing the traditional feminine role: she is a bystander, a person on the sidelines, who is talked about but who does not actually participate in the action in the joke. This is so even though her lesbianism is the basis for the punch line.

This brings us to the end of our survey. I have tried to suggest how each perspective, discipline, and methodology (or whatever) might make sense of the joke about the three brothers in the bar. Each perspective examines a different facet of the joke, and while a joke may not be completely illuminated by a given perspective, it does offer important insights that, when put together with other ones, does a good job of explaining and interpreting the joke in a relatively complete and interesting manner.

Humor is Serious but Not Solemn

James Thurber offers an important insight about humor. Discussing playwrights, Thurber wrote:

> The modern morbid playwrights seen to have fallen for the fake argument that only tragedy is serious and has importance....the truth is that comedy is just as important, and often more serious in its approach to truth, and what few writers seem to realize or admit, usually more difficult to write. (Gartner, 1981)

It is much more difficult to make people laugh than it is to make people cry. We can make people cry by writing a tragedy and pulling on their heartstrings. This can be done in a million ways. All we have to do is create believable characters and then destroy them.

But it is a much different and infinitely more difficult thing to amuse people and make them laugh. Take the case of stand-up comedians, for example. It often takes comedians years to work up an hour's worth of good material. These comedians might seem to be at ease and their material might seem to be coming right off the top of their heads, but that seldom is the case. Comedians are always terrified about "bombing" and always suffer from great anxiety.

It is because of the difficulty in creating humorous material that comedy shows on television often have a number of writers, who collaborate on the shows. In some cases, such as *Your Show of Shows,* you get, by chance, a remarkable pool of writers and gifted performers, and you have a great success. More often, however, the writers are mediocre and even though the performers may be talented, the shows are failures. Talented performers need good material and if they don't get it, their shows don't last very long.

Thurber's second point deals with the theater (and other media by implication). He argues that comedies are often more serious in their approach to truth than tragedies. Because we have learned (from the Puritans?) to assume that things that taste good are bad for us and that things that taste bad are good for us, and that things that amuse us and make us laugh are of minor concern, we assume that we only find out about life from serious works such as tragedies (and the tragic mode in other media). I think we can make a distinction between solemnity and seriousness. Some people are very solemn, but they are not necessarily serious at all; they may not have a thought in their head and may, instead, be depressed, inhibited, whatever. Other people clown around a good deal of the time and are very humorous. They can also be very serious. The Zen masters, many centuries ago, taught by joking, clowning around, and sometimes even dressing like clowns.

An Author's Hope

I hope that you will find this book entertaining—in the best sense of the term. I hope that you will learn something, pick up some interesting ideas, get some new insights and, at the same time, enjoy the jokes and other humor in the book. Writing about humor is often rather deadly and some works on humor are humorless. When you anatomize a joke, you kill it—but I do this only after I've "told" you the joke and you've had an opportunity to be amused by it.

So I don't feel bad about analyzing jokes and other forms of humor, and, in fact, I like to think that in dealing with the ways different disciplines make sense of humor, I've offered my readers the best of both worlds: I've explained certain aspects of a number of disciplines (and scholarly perspectives) and I've offered some good examples of humor.

It occurs to me that this book may be of use, then, to a several groups of people. First, and primarily, I hope my book will appeal to anyone (scholar, layperson, professional humorist) interested in humor. I also hope this book will be of use to those interested in multidisciplinary or interdisciplinary approaches to topics (professors who might teach courses in the social sciences, the humanities, and in areas such as cultural criticism). This book uses elements from a number of different disciplines to analyze, interpret, and explain jokes and humor, in general.

A number of years ago I was on sabbatical in England and went to a conference on popular culture at one of the universities there. I got into a conversation with a professor and mentioned I used a multidisciplined approach in my work. "Here," he said, "we call it undisciplined." Whether that is the case with this book is something that you will have to decide.

References

Brewer, John, and Albert Hunter. *Multimethod Research: A Synthesis of Styles.* Newbury Park, CA: Sage Publications, 1989.

Chapman, Tony, and Hugh Foot, eds. *Humor and Laughter: Theory Research and Applications.* London: John Wiley & Sons, 1976.

Eco, Umberto. *The Role of the Reader.* Bloomington: Indiana University Press, 1984.

Gartner, Michael. "The Hard Work Behind Thurber's Humor." *Wall Street Journal,* 27 November 1981.

Hinsie, Leland E., and Robert Jean Cambell, eds. *Psychiatric Dictionary* (Fourth Edition). New York: Oxford University Press, 1970.

Lodge, David, ed. *Modern Criticism and Theory.* London: Longman, 1988.

*Humor ameliorates deprivation. But not
through some substituting or pacifying agent.
It is not a distractive Roman carnival to take
the mind of the populace off its troubles.
Humor ameliorates as the result of its special
"miracle" characteristics. These characteristics combine to make humor a microcosm
of transition between alone and together.
Humor provides simultaneous involvement in
these states.*

*Humor is generally—not invariably, but
generally—shared with other persons....
People are amused together; they laugh
together. Their mirth is potentiated by the
mirth of others, with whom it is shared; their
laughter is potentiated by the laughter of
those laughing with them. The social nature
of humor is most obvious in the comedy of
cultures and other group entities. Here,
humor is found to play a dynamic role in the
very evolution of the group, offering
powerful mechanisms whereby the group
unfolds its destiny.*

> —William F. Fry and Melanie Allen
> *Make 'Em Laugh: Life Studies
> of Comedy Writers*

2

The Messages of Mirth:
Humor and Communication Theory

Because we find humor so enjoyable, we seldom consider that humor also communicates information to us. After all, most of the humor we are exposed to is based on language—spoken by joke tellers and stand-up comedians, actors and actresses in plays and films, or characters in cartoons and comic strips. (There are also, of course, physical and visual humor, which are dealt with in my discussion of semiotics and graphic or visual humor.)

In the first chapter I discussed the problem raised by the "reader-response" theorists, described my orientation as a multidisciplinary one, and sketched out how individuals, from a number of different disciplines, might analyze a joke. Now, in this chapter, I deal with humor from a very broad perspective—that of communication studies, itself a multidisciplinary field. After this analysis, we move on to more disciplinary-specific studies—remembering, all the time, that I am offering interpretations that are, in essence, case studies that represent the views of particular individuals who use a discipline or methodology, and am not trying to suggest that I show how everyone in a given discipline or everyone who uses a particular methodology would analyze humor.

The Matter of Jokes

Let's take jokes as an example. I suggest that telling jokes, which are commonly defined as narratives with punch lines told to amuse and generate laughter, is not the best way to be funny. It is much better, I argue, to use some of the basic techniques of humor, such as exaggeration, irony, facetiousness, and parody, to create your own humor. But telling jokes is a common way for people to amuse others; actually, when we tell jokes we are giving low-key performances, retelling the jokes that others have told us.

The fact that jokes have punch lines leads to an important insight. John R. Pierce and A. Michael Noll, in their book *Signals: The Science of Telecommunications* (Scientific American Library, 1990) point out that there is a connection between unpredictability and information. They write, discussing Claude Shannon's theory of information: "The degree to which messages from a source are unpredictable is taken as a measure of the amount of information in such messages" (1990, 56). What this suggests is that jokes, which are based on punch lines, that are by nature unpredictable, contain a great deal of information. The punch line, remember, leads to a resolution of the joke narrative that is surprising and unexpected.

Humor, in its various forms, can be seen as involving messages transmitted from one source to another. Let me adopt a famous model of communication, or, more precisely, speech acts, elaborated by Roman Jakobson, to make this clearer. A diagram of his model follows:

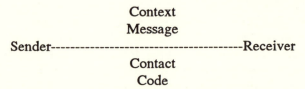

In this model we find a sender (the person telling a joke, for instance) sending a message (the joke) to a receiver (someone else, such as people listening to the joke).

The message is sent through a contact, which we can say is analogous to a medium (spoken word, radio, television, etc.), and is delivered in a code (the English language or some subcode of the language, such as academic discourse, legal discourse, etc.). This message is delivered in a certain context and makes reference to that context, what might be described as the understandings and cultural background of the person sending the message and the people receiving it. In the case of a joke, this message is affected by such things as facial expression, body language, and accents used. So we are dealing with a rather complex phenomenon here; the message itself is broader or more involved than the meaning of the message, per se.

As Jakobson described this model:

> [T]he *addresser* sends a *message* to the *addressee*. To be operative the message requires a *context* referred to, seizable by the addressee, and either verbal or capable of being verbalized; a *code* fully, or at least partially, common to the addresser and addressee; and, finally, a *contact*, a physical channel and psychological connection between the addresser and addressee, enabling both of them to enter and stay in communication. (1969, 353)

Humor, we might say, is a kind of message that is communicated in various forms (such as jokes, cartoons, parodies, situation comedies, etc.) that involves senders (writers, cartoonists, comedians, etc. who generate the messages) and receivers (audiences who need to decode or interpret the messages "correctly" in order to laugh). These messages are mediated (spoken word, radio, television, film, drawings, facial expressions, and body language).

Play Frames and Humor

It is important that audiences recognize that the messages intended to generate mirth and laughter are to be construed as humorous ones. What happens, according to some communication theorists, is that play frames are established that tell audiences "this is meant to be funny and not taken seriously." As William Fry, Jr., writes in *Sweet Madness: A Study of Humor:*

> During the unfolding of humor, one is suddenly confronted by an explicit-implicit reversal when the punch line is delivered. The reversal helps distinguish humor from play, dreams, etc. Sudden reversals such as characterize the punch line moment in humor are disruptive and foreign to play, etc....But the reversal also has the unique effect of forcing upon the humor participants an internal redefining of reality. Inescapably, the punch line combines communication and metacommunication. (1968, 153)

Humor is different from play, according to Fry, and always involves people recognizing that some kind of a metacommunication is taking place.

Consider irony, for example. In irony one says something that is meant to be taken in the opposite manner from the literal content of the statement. Irony is often misunderstood by people who do not recognize that the tone of a speaker or writer or other circumstances connected to written material, for instance, are telling them "don't take this seriously." So irony is very dangerous and ironic statements are frequently misinterpreted.

With jokes the situation is different. When people tell jokes, they generally announce that they are telling a joke, so that the people listening to the joke will establish the required play frame and not take the communication seriously. When we watch stand-up comedians on television, we know that we are listening to humorists and interpret what they say by adopting a play-frame perspective. The very identity of the stand-up comedian establishes, automatically, a play frame.

Bateson on Humor

Gregory Bateson, one of the most important communication theorists of recent years, suggests that humor is connected to paradox. (William Fry, who was discussed above, was a member of one of Bateson's research teams, as a matter of fact.) Laughter, Bateson reminds us, is one of three common convulsive behaviors found in people, along with grief and orgasm. These convulsions, along with those of epilepsy and shock therapy, have a common characteristic, he argues: there is a buildup, what is called a "tonic" phase in which tension builds up; something happens (such as, in the case of jokes, a story with a punch line is told) and then "something happens, and the organism begins quaking, heaving, oscillating, especially about the diaphragm" ("The Position of Humor in Human Communication," from *Cybernetics,* quoted in Levine, 1969).

Of the three kinds of convulsive behavior, laughter is the one that Bateson believes has the clearest ideational content. He writes:

> It is relatively easy to discuss what a joke is, what are the characteristics that make a joke, what is the point of a joke. The sort of analysis that I want to propose assumes that the messages in the first phase of telling the joke are such that while the informational content is, so to speak, on the surface, the other content types in various forms are implicit in the background. When the point of a joke is reached, suddenly this background material is brought into attention and a paradox, or something like it is touched off. A circuit of contradictory notions is completed. (Levine, 162)

Not only do we find paradoxes in jokes, Bateson continues, but they are the "prototypic paradigm" for humor of all kinds and laughter only takes place when a paradoxical circuit is completed.

This is understandable in terms of Bateson's belief that "paradoxes are the stuff of human communication" (Levine, 164). These paradoxes, he adds, are an important ingredient in comfortable human relations, psychotherapeutic change, and humor; in all three we find the presence and acceptance of paradoxes, which give freedom, which he contrasts with the "rigidity" of logic. Humor is connected to paradoxes and ultimately to freedom, which explains why Bateson sees humor as having therapeutic implications. The punch line in a joke leads us in directions we had not anticipated and suggests that there is an element of freedom and chance in our lives. This, in turn, suggests changes are possible and that we need not be prisoners of our habits, fixations, and so on.

There is another thinker, Arthur Koestler, whose theories are somewhat similar to Fry's notions about play frames and the interaction of the implicit and explicit and to Bateson's theories of paradox. Koestler ties humor to the linkage of two contrasting phenomena, a process that he calls "bisociation."

Bisociation and Humor

In his book *Insight and Outlook: An Inquiry into the Common Foundations of Science, Art and Social Ethics* (Macmillan, 1949) Koestler suggests that humor is caused by intersecting fields. This process, he tells us, involves *"any mental occurrence simultaneously associated with two habitually incompatible contexts"* (1949, 37). Bisociation, he adds, is not the same thing as ambiguity; the two fields that come together in bisociation are generally seen as incompatible ones, and they don't really come together at the same time but, instead, "oscillate." And once these disparate phenomena bisociate, they lose their identity and coalesce into something else. That's why, he points out, jokes are only funny the first time we hear them. Koestler suggests that bisociation is at the root of humor and writes:

> The necessary and sufficient conditions which define the nature of the comic stimulus are the sudden bisociation of a junctional idea or event with two independent operative fields, and the presence of a dominant aggressive component in the compound emotional charge.
>
> The resulting abrupt transfer of thought from one field to the other causes a momentary dissociation of parts of the emotional charge from its thought-context, and the discharge of this redundant energy in the laughter reflex.
>
> Sustained humor results from a sustained bisociation of a character or situation. The narrative in this case moves through a series of junctional situations, oscillating between the two fields. (1949, 110)

We have, then, two separate fields that come together in something that contains, somehow, aspects of both fields. What Koestler calls the higher forms of the comic—satire and irony, for example—are also generated by a bisociative clash that disrupts the fields connected to implicit habits of thought, ridiculing conventions and habits. There is, we must note, an aggressive aspect to the comic in Koestler's theory.

Koestler believes that original creative activity of all sorts, not only humor, is based on bisociation. His notion of different operative fields coming together and bisociating is also related to the notion of incongruity, one of the major theories used to explain humor. Incongruity involves something happening that was not intended, something happening that could not be anticipated, some kind of a strange combination of elements. He devotes a number of chapters to humor, laughter, the comic, and related matters in the book and also returns to the subject at the end of the book, when he discusses the theories of Bergson (of whom he is very critical) and Freud (who he admires, for the most part, but with whom he differs on a number of points).

Figure and Ground

People must have a common frame of reference or what might be called a knowledge base in order to interpret the communication correctly. Jakobson calls this a "context." Without a common frame of reference, one cannot understand allusions and cannot recognize from a humorist's tone that a statement is not to be interpreted literally or taken seriously. This frame of reference is, to a large degree, generated by our folklore and mass media, which are some of the basic ways that people in modern societies are socialized.

A humorous text can be seen as a "figure" that is understood against the "ground" of a given society and culture and the knowledge base of the people in it. In the figure-ground relationship, each element helps define the other. The ground (in this case, our beliefs, values, cultural and social history) gives the figure (the humor) a base to work on and the humor, the figure, helps shape the ground.

Let's consider a very famous joke here:

A couple goes to a child psychiatrist with a problem. "We have two children," they tell the psychiatrist. "One is incurably pessimistic, always complaining and seeing the worst in things. The other is incurably optimistic. Is there some way I can

change them so they aren't so extreme?" "I've got the solution," says the psychia-
trist. "This is what you do. You take the pessimistic child and put him in a room
with all the toys he might possibly want to play with and all the good things he
might want to eat—ice cream, pies, cakes, etc.—and with a butler and maid who
will look after his every need. Put the optimistic child in a room with a great deal of
horse manure and a shovel. Keep them in those rooms for a month and then come
back and tell me how things are going." A month later the couple returns to the
child psychiatrist. "What happened?" asks the psychiatrist. "It didn't work," says
the father. "We did everything you said, but after a month our pessimistic son, in
the room with all the toys and good things to eat, hadn't changed. He was moody
and depressed. He said he was worried that some day he'd have to leave the room."
"And what about the optimistic child?" asked the psychiatrist. "It didn't work with
him. When we went to see him in his room he was as happy as can be and digging
away like crazy." "How come?" asked the psychiatrist. "If there's all this horseshit
here," our son said, "there has to be a pony somewhere."

This joke involves certain stock figures in American comicdom: psychiatrists, troubled parents, and their children, who are a problem or
"difficult" for one reason or another.

When we hear this joke, because it is a joke we know that the situation described is not to be taken seriously. We don't feel any sense of
anxiety about the fact that a psychiatrist is involved in a family difficulty. But we don't know how the comic situation will be resolved. There
are two punch lines in this joke. One involves the pessimistic child who
is afraid his good fortune will come to an end and defeats the plan of the
psychiatrist and his parents, who have conspired with the psychiatrist;
the other involves the optimistic child who assumes that the abundance
of horse manure in his room indicates that there has to be a pony somewhere and also defeats the plans of the psychiatrist.

Both children have, in different ways, stymied the psychiatrist and
their parents; this theme of children outwitting adults is also an important one in our "child-centered" American culture. The joke also reaf-
firms a sense many people have that it is difficult to change people's
natures and ridicules psychiatrists, diminishing the fear that some people
hold for them.

When we call psychiatrists "shrinks" we are finding a way to deal
with our anxiety about them; we deal with this anxiety by "shrinking"
the psychiatrists, which has the effect of making us seem larger and
more powerful. The joke also pokes fun at the reliance many parents
in America have on so-called experts, and the desire many parents
have to shape and, somehow, control their children and produce
"superchildren."

Aberrant Decoding

Communication theorists suggest that audiences of mass-mediated texts (television shows, movies, etc.) often "decode" or interpret these texts incorrectly—that is, in ways different from the ways the creators of the texts wanted them to be decoded. (This topic was dealt with, in part, earlier in the discussion of reader-response theorists and humor.) There are a number of reasons for this aberrant decoding. The encoders, the writers and artists, come from different economic and social backgrounds than their audience; the writers probably are better educated than their audiences, have different reference frames, and make allusions to matters and phenomena (such as books, characters in plays, historical personalities) that the audiences often don't recognize. In addition, everyone sees the world from different perspectives, based on where one is brought up, one's class level, one's personality, experiences, and so forth. Thus, there are good reasons to expect that audiences will decode texts aberrantly.

How, then, do you maintain the aberrant decoding thesis when large numbers of people at a film, for example, laugh at precisely the same time at something characters in the film do or say? If the audience "gets" the humor, doesn't that suggest that people do not decode texts as aberrantly as the communication theorists suggest they do? Or can it be that members of an audience decode a humorous text aberrantly, but still manage to understand a good deal of the message? If it were the case that each member of the audience had his or her own distinctive sense of humor, how do you explain a group response of laughter to something in a film or play or something a stand-up comedian says?

The answer might be that while each of us has a distinct sense of humor, we share certain commonalities that strike us as funny—probably on a class-based level. Comedians have told me that sometimes they have to adapt their humor and if cerebral humor or routines based on allusions and word play, for instance, aren't going over with a working-class audience, a shift to toilet humor is often effective.

I can remember watching a Marx brothers film in Paris at the Cite Universitaire. The audience, composed of students from many different countries, laughed hysterically throughout the film. So there are probably some codes that are international in scope while others are national, regional, local, as well as class based or based on ethnicity or something else like that. You have to know the scene in San Francisco, for example, to recognize that allusions in jokes about the Castro district refer to the gays and lesbians who live there, in a homosexual enclave, so to speak.

Humor about Communications Problems

Our inability to communicate with one another clearly is, itself, the subject of much humor. The following joke is an example of this.

A woman goes to a lawyer and says she wants to divorce her husband. "Do you have grounds?" asks the lawyer. "Yes," says the woman. "Six acres." "Do you have a grudge?" asks the lawyer. "No," says the woman. "We have a carport." I'd better get more specific, thinks the lawyer. "Does he beat you?" asks the lawyer. "No," says the woman. "I get up before he does." "Well, why do you want to get divorced?" asks the lawyer. "Because my husband doesn't understand me," replies the woman.

The punch line is based on a reversal—on the woman's inability to understand every question asked of her. Thus, there is something ironic to her statement that she wants a divorce because her husband doesn't understand her; nobody could, we are led to infer.

This joke is based, among other things, on the technique of misunderstanding, of not interpreting verbal statements correctly, which is one of the more common techniques used to generate humor. It is not the same technique as mistakes, which are based on erroneous actions. A mistake is something we do; a misunderstanding is something we think.

Humor and Interpersonal Communication

Because humor often involves misunderstandings, it can be argued that humor often plays an important role in preventing people who dislike one another, or should dislike one another, from recognizing their true feelings and acting on these feelings. Humor can mystify and cloud interpersonal relationships and thus, by masking differences and fostering miscommunication, may have salutary effects.

Humor also downgrades the seriousness with which we take things and thus tends to dilute hostile and poisonous feelings people sometimes feel toward one another. Humor also defuses poisonous, or potentially poisonous relationships, by allowing people to release their anger and energy in relatively harmless ways, often on substitute victims.

Humor can also distract people and divert their attention from being focused, in a negative and hostile way, on an individual or a group of individuals. That is, it can divert attention onto more or less "acceptable" scapegoats, the characters in jokes and cartoons who become functional alternatives or, in theatrical parlance, "stand ins," for the real world targets of a person's hostility and anger. Sometimes, of course, jokes and other forms of humor are directed at ethnic, religious, and racial groups and reinforce stereotypes and negative images, and in these cases, the humor might be described as harmful or socially dysfunctional. But as far as interpersonal relationships are concerned, in general, humor often plays an important role in distracting people, defusing hostility and anger, and thus often diminishing person-to-person hostility.

Conclusions

Humor, we see, is an extremely complicated phenomenon that works in mysterious ways and is of great value to us, even when, at times, it hampers communication or prevents us from interpreting messages correctly. The jokes we tell may seem relatively simple, and they may be simple in some cases, but understanding how they work, the way they are connected to play frames and paradoxes, to cognition, and to our knowledge base, for example, suggests that they are much more complicated than we imagine them to be. One of the paradoxes of humor is that we have been fascinated with it for thousands of years, we crave it (and reward our great humorists with great acclaim and wealth), and yet we still don't understand very well how humor works and why we laugh.

In the chapter on philosophical approaches to humor that follows, I consider a problem philosophers have dealt with over the years, the nature of humor and "why" we laugh. Then, in the chapter after that, on rhetorical theory, I move from "why" theories down the ladder of abstraction and deal with "what makes us laugh." I offer a list of forty-five techniques, which, I suggest, are used by humorists to generate laughter and offer examples that show how a number of these techniques work.

References

Fry, William. *Sweet Madness: A Study of Humor*. Palo Alto, CA: Pacific Books, 1968.
Jakobson, Roman. "Linguistics and Poetics." In *Style in Language*, edited by T. Sebeok. Cambridge, MA: MIT Press, 1960.

Koestler, Arthur. *Insight and Outlook: An Inquiry into the Common Foundations of Science, Art and Social Ethics.* New York: Macmillan, 1949.

Levine, Jacob, ed. *Motivation in Humor.* New York: Atherton Press, 1969.

Pierce, John R., and A. Michael Noll. *Signals: The Science of Telecommunications.* New York: Scientific American Library, 1990.

Wittgenstein said that a philosophy book could be written consisting of nothing but jokes: these would be based on fallacies, category mistakes, and other confusions about the logic of different concepts and arguments. We can even read certain humorous works not intended as philosophy books, such as Lewis Carroll's Alice in Wonderland *and* Through the Looking Glass, *and find many philosophical lessons.*

—John Morreall
The Philosophy of Laughter and Humor

3

The Problem of Laughter:
Philosophical Approaches to Humor

From Aristotle's time to the present, philosophers have been interested in what humor is and have devoted a considerable amount of attention to the subject. As a rule, they have worked at a relatively high level of abstraction and focused their speculations on the nature of humor, on what humor is rather than on its social significance or specific techniques of humor, and things like that. In this chapter we deal with speculations about the nature of humor and why people laugh; this will be followed by a chapter on rhetorical approaches that is much more pragmatic and considers what makes people laugh.

Aristotle on Comedy

Aristotle saw "poetry" (by which he meant, we might say, literary works in general) as based on imitation and argues for a mimetic theory of the arts. As he writes in *De Poetica*:

> Epic poetry and Tragedy, as also Comedy, Dithyrambic poetry, and most flute-playing and lyre-playing, are all, viewed as a whole, modes of imitation. But at the same time they differ from one another in three ways, either by difference of kind in their means, or by differences in the objects or manner of their imitations (McKeon, 1941, 1455).

The difference between tragedy and comedy for Aristotle is that "the one would make its personages worse, and the other better, than the men of the present day" (1941, 1456). This imitation, he argues, is "natural to man" and offers him an advantage over the animals in that man is "the most imitative creature in the world" (1941, 1457).

The difference between comedy and tragedy, Aristotle continues, is that comedy is:

> an imitation of men worse than average; worse, however, not as regards any sort of fault, but only as regards one particular kind, the Ridiculous, which is a species of the Ugly. The Ridiculous may be defined as a mistake or deformity not productive of pain or harm to others; the mask, for instance, that excites laughter, is something ugly and distorted without causing pain. (1941, 1459)

Comedy originates, Aristotle tells us, in improvisations of phallic songs. After a long period of evolution, the songs led to comic revels. These then became dramatic works, in which the characters acted out the story. When the archon officially granted playwrights a chorus of comedians (who replaced volunteers) a historic record of comic poets began, says Aristotle.

For Aristotle, then, humor is natural to man, is tied to imitation (as is all drama), and, specifically, to the imitation of men who are worse than average, men who are, somehow, ridiculous. Aristotle's ideas about comedy being based on an imitation of men who are ridiculous, who are inferior to others, is at the heart of the superiority theory of humor. This theory suggests that all humor is connected to the sense of superiority the person laughing feels about the person or persons laughed at.

Hobbes and Superiority

Various other philosophers have elaborated theories that tie humor to superiority, the most famous one being that of Hobbes. In Hobbes's *Leviathan* there is a discussion of laughter that is often quoted in books on humor. Hobbes writes that humor arises from a "sudden glory arising from a sudden comparison of some eminency in ourselves, by comparison with the infirmity of others, or with our own formerly" (quoted in Arthur Koestler, *Insight and Outlook*, MacMillan, 1949, 56). In chapter 6, part 1 of *Leviathan,* he describes his notions of sudden glory and laughter in more detail. He writes:

> *Sudden-glory,* is the passion which maketh those *grimaces* called LAUGHTER; and is caused either by some sudden act of their own, that pleaseth them; or by apprehension of some deformed thing in another, by comparison whereof they suddenly applaud themselves. And it is incident most to them, that are conscious of the fewest abilities in themselves; who are forced to keep themselves in their own favour, by observing the imperfections of other men. And therefore much laughter

at the defects of others, is a sign of pusillanimity. For of great minds, one of the proper works is, to help and free others from scorn; and compare themselves only with the most able. (1957, 36)

This offers a slightly different perspective on humor from the first Hobbes quotation, which is the one most commonly found in books on humor, though I've not been able to find it in *Leviathan,* I must confess.

Hobbes suggests here that there is an element of feeling inferior that is found in those who seek out humor the most; they attempt to preserve a sense of their superiority by looking for imperfections in others. So laughter at the "defects" of other people is a sign of pusillanimity or what we would call a sense of inferiority or weakness. Superiority is always, then, something felt relative to others; one may feel superior to some and inferior to others, and assuage this sense of relative inferiority by finding those inferior to oneself at whom one can laugh (just as those superior to us are laughing at us, we must presume).

The opposite of sudden glory for Hobbes is sudden dejection, which leads to weeping instead of laughter. Both, Hobbes argues, are "sudden motions," since, as he puts it, "no man laughs at old jests; or weeps for an old calamity" (1957, 36). There is, then, for Hobbes, an element of newness or suddenness that is tied to laughter, as well as a sense of relative superiority. Humor, then, would give momentary relief to those who feel relatively low down on the totem pole or great chain of being, but gain pleasure by realizing that although there are some above them, there are others below or beneath them.

Let us turn now to another theory of humor held by a philosopher, Søren Kierkegaard, one of the fathers of existential thought, who saw the absurd aspects of life as the basis of comedy.

Kierkegaard and the Absurd

In an appendix to a book on comedy (long essays by Meredith and Bergson) Wylie Sypher (1956, 196) discusses the ideas of Kierkegaard. Sypher uses the term *comedy* but he is really talking about humor, as we understand it. His conception of comedy is so broad that it permeates existence; the comic is not merely a part of life for Sypher but life is comic, as he sees things. He quotes Kierkegaard in this respect: "the comical is present in every stage of life, for wherever there is life there is contradiction, and wherever there is contradiction the comical is present." It is not a big leap from the absurd in comedy to the existential conception of the absurd in life or life as absurd.

This notion that life is, somehow, absurd, can be looked upon as one of the central tenets of existentialism. Existential absurdity stems from the alleged stupidity and chaos of life, of modern man's dissociated sensibilities, and of confusions that bring comedy close to tragedy. As Sypher explains things, tragedy and comedy merge:

> [T]he direst calamities that befall man seem to prove that human life at its depths is inherently absurd. The comic and the tragic views of life no longer exclude each other. Perhaps the most important discovery of modern criticism is the perception that comedy and tragedy are somehow akin, or that comedy can tell us many things about our situation even tragedy cannot. (1956, 193)

Tragedy is, in a sense, much more limited than comedy, being focused on the ineluctable destruction of some great figure. It is comedy, Sypher tells us, that brings the disorderly aspects of existence into art in a century of irrationalism and disorder.

As Sypher explains:

> Wherever man has been able to think about his present plight he has felt "the suction of the absurd." He has been forced to see himself in unheroic positions. In his sanest moments the modern hero is aware that he is J. Alfred Prufrock, or Osric, an attendant lord—"Almost, at times, the fool." Or else Sweeney, the apeneck, seeking low pleasures while death and the raven drift above.

> We have, in short, been forced to admit that the absurd is more than ever inherent in human existence: that is, the irrational, the inexplicable, the surprising, the nonsensical—in other words, the comic. (1956, 195)

The gap between our reason and capacity for good and our brutality and propensity for evil is inexplicable, Sypher suggests, without the conception of absurdity as central to life.

From the existential perspective, life moves toward *reductio ad absurdem*—and it is comedy, not tragedy, which best explains this situation. Tragedy is always "high" Sypher argues, but comedy can range between high and low. It is often difficult, he cautions, to separate the comic from the tragic, since some comedies don't lead to laughter and some tragedies are hysterically funny. There is, of course, the tragicomedy, in which the two are fused together, but in this is a bastard form, Sypher believes, since it is the tragedy that is central and comedy is used, from time to time, for relief. What complicates matters is that it is very difficult, Sypher suggests, to find satisfactory definitions of either comedy or tragedy.

Sypher mentions some of the most important theories of laughter, which claim it is based on one of the following: malice, release from restraint, response to the incongruous or the improper, ambivalence (attraction and repulsion to a situation), and bewilderment. He mentions Hobbes's theory that humor is based on superiority and Ludovici's notion that laughter is a sign of superior adaptation in humans—who smile, instead of showing their fangs (the way dogs and other wild animals do) when they are threatened.

He also discusses Lamb's theory that laughter arises from an overflow of sympathy, Schopenhauer's view that laughter is a frenzy that stems from a sudden perception of incongruity between our ideals and actualities, and Nietzsche's idea that laughter is a frenzy that stems from pain and fury. None of these theories, Sypher argues, is adequate to explain humor and, to make matters worse, there is no agreement among theorists about what comedy or laughter is or how they work. Despite these difficulties, Sypher does believe it is possible to make distinctions about the various kinds of humor and see how humor relates to society—a subject that takes us away from our concern with philosophical matters and one that we will not deal with here.

Let us turn now to another important philosophical theory of humor, that of the great French philosopher Bergson, who elaborated his theory in his book *Le Rire* or *Laughter*.

Bergson on Humor: The Problem of the Mechanical

Henri Bergson published his book *Laughter* in 1900, forty-one years before his death. It is one of the more important efforts by a philosopher toward understanding the nature of humor and related matters such as humor and comedy. Bergson starts off quite logically, arguing in his first chapter on "The Comic in General" that humor "does not exist outside the pale of what is strictly *human*" (Sypher, 1956, 62). For example, landscapes are never laughable. When we laugh at something inanimate, he adds, it is always because of some resemblance in the object to man or to some use to which men put the object. There is always a human connection.

When we laugh at a person who is the victim of a practical joke, it is similar to laughing at a person who falls—what produces the laughter in both cases is "a certain *mechanical inelasticity,* just where one would expect to find the wideawake adaptability and the living pliableness of a human being" (Sypher, 1956, 67). This situation is similar in nature to characters who are rigid, in terms of their ideas and are inflexible—and are unaware of this quality. Their rigidity is the source of their being comic and laughter is the social corrective that people use in responding to this rigidity.

At the center of Bergson's theory is the idea that comedy involves, as he puts it, "*Something mechanical encrusted on the living*" (Sypher, 1956, 84). This is, he suggests, a central image that can lead the theorist in a number of different directions. For example, in his chapter "The Comic Element in Movements" he writes: "The attitudes, gestures and movements of the human body are laughable in exact proportion as that body reminds us of a mere machine" (Sypher, 1956, 79). That is, when the body imitates a machine and thus is rigid and has the mechanical "encrusted" on it, so to speak, the body becomes something comic. He adds, "We laugh every time a person gives us the impression of being a thing" (Sypher, 1956, 97).

As examples he offers Sancho Panza being tossed in the air like a football and Baron Munchausen being turned into a cannon ball and shot through space. In both cases, a human being is, in a sense, turned into a thing and thus rendered comic.

Next, he moves onto comic situations and asserts:

> Any arrangement of acts and events is comic which gives us, in a single combination, the illusion of life and the distinct impression of a mechanical arrangement. (Sypher, 1956, 105)

Thus, a jack-in-the-box is comic because it is a mechanical device that seems to have the characteristics of a human—motion, resilience, and so on. He also discusses scenes in plays in which there is a conflict between a fixated and thus "mechanical" character and a regular, rounded, flexible person.

Bergson uses this same principle in dealing with language. He suggests that a comic effect is always produced when an individual takes literally an expression that was used figuratively. In this case, taking an expression literally is the equivalent of acting in a nonthinking, nonflexible, mechanical way. In addition, there is the element of transposition to consider. He writes: "A comic effect is always obtainable by transposing the natural expression of an idea into another key" (Sypher, 1956, 140).

For example, if we transpose the solemn into the familiar, we get parody—and this has led some philosophers, he adds, to suggest that all comedy is tied to degradation. But, cautions Bergson, degradation is only one form of transposition and transposition is only one way of generating laughter, so it is too reductionistic. One can also transpose the small into the large, yielding exaggeration, another subcategory of humor—but also not a concept large enough to cover all comedy.

In his discussion of comedy of character, he suggests that as far as the comic is concerned, the character of a figure in a text is not particularly important, but that unsociability is. Bergson sums up his discussion of comedy and character as follows:

> Whether a character is good or bad is of little moment; granted he is unsociable, he is capable of becoming comic. We now see that the seriousness of the case is of no importance either: whether serious or trifling, it is still capable of making us laugh, providing care be taken not to arouse our emotions. Unsociability in the performer and insensibility in the spectator—such, in a word, are the two essential conditions. (Sypher, 1956, 154–55)

There is, he adds, a third condition implicit in these two, namely, the matter of automatism. "What is essentially laughable is what is done automatically," he writes (Sypher, 1956, 155). He is talking here about such things as involuntary gestures, unconscious remarks, absentmindedness, contradicting oneself, and so on.

Ultimately, he adds, "every comic character is a *type*. Inversely, every resemblance to a type has something comic in it" (Sypher, 1956, 156). And comedy, he continues, in dealing with general types, is the only art that deals with the general, deals with types of people we know and have met. As proof he cites the titles of two comedies—*The Misanthrope* and *The Miser*. These fixated or one-dimensional characters, dominated by a particular humor, find themselves victims of strange compulsions and, in their mad singlemindedness, remind us of characters in dreams. Comic absurdity, he suggests, has the same nature as our dreams.

There is something ironic, if you think about it, about Bergson's ideas on humor. His whole theory of comedy is built upon one central notion—on the relationship between the mechanical and the living being the core of comedy. Yet his theory itself has a certain rigidity of structure to it in that it derives all aspects of comedy with undeviating logic from one central notion. As such, it may be somewhat mechanistic itself, if not reductionistic and simplistic. Nevertheless, Bergson has offered an interesting and powerful theory of the comic and, at the same time, has pointed out a number of different techniques that humorists use to create humor—such as exaggeration, over-literalness, and rigidity. All humor may not involve the mechanical and the living but, as Bergson demonstrates rather convincingly, a great deal of it does.

Bergson has been identified as an "incongruity" theorist—arguing that, in essence, all humor is tied, one way or another, to incongruities. This theory is, I would suggest, the most commonly held general theory of humor.

Incongruity Theories

A good case can be made that Bergson's ideas suggest that humor is really tied to incongruity. This theory says that all humor is based on some kind of a surprising difference between what we expect and what we get. For example, consider Bergson's theory. We expect people to be flexible and reasonable, he argues, and when we find characters who are rigid and "mechanical," we find this comic. In essence, we are experiencing an element of incongruity.

Another philosopher who can be identified with incongruity theories of humor is Immanuel Kant, who argued that the enjoyment of jokes yields pleasure, not the experience of beauty. Pleasure, we must assume, is something relatively superficial and momentary, unlike beauty, which is profound and long lasting. He adds that "laughter is an affection arising from the sudden transformation of a strained expectation into nothing" (Piddington, 1963, 168). It is important, Kant points out, that the comic transformation does not lead to the opposite of the strained expectation (for that might cause grief), but leads to nothing. This notion that a strained expectation leads to nothing is, I would suggest, another example of an incongruity theory. You expect something and you get, Kant tells us, nothing, and this generates "enjoyment for a moment" and laughter.

Schopenhauer spells out the incongruity theory more directly. He writes:

> The cause of laughter in every case is simply the sudden perception of the incongruity between a concept and the real objects which have been thought through it

in some relation, and laughter itself is just the expression of this incongruity. (Piddington, 1963, 171-72)

Here, the notion of incongruity is directly asserted as the cause of all laughter, though it is based on a "sudden perception," which suggests that the time dimension is of some significance and that laughter is connected to some kind of a shock. In jokes this sudden perception would be created by the punch line or in other kinds of humor by some foolish actions undertaken by some individual.

On the Ontological Status of Humor

In this discussion of philosophical theories of humor, nothing has been said about the ontological status of humor. That is, does humor exist in the real world (assuming we can know this real world) or is it in the mind of the laugher or beholder? Chapman and Foot argue that it is wrong to confuse humor with laughter, suggest that nothing is funny for everyone and anything is potentially funny for someone, attack a number of theories of humor and deny that what is conventionally called a sense of humor exists (1976). This leads to the following conclusion:

> We deny then that a sense of humour, thus defined, exists. To deny that a sense of humor exists is not of course to deny that humour exists. But where does humour exist? *Humour lies neither in laughter nor in jokes but only in the minds of men.* ...In other words, humour is a mental experience—an O in the model S-O-R. Laughter is an R; a joke is an S. (1976, 83)

The O in this formula stands for the organism, that is, a human being.

This notion that humor is a mental experience, that it involves the mind, is not difficult to accept. After all, one has to perceive an incongruity or recognize one's superiority (or inferiority), and these phenomena take place in the mind. In a sense, all theories of humor and the comic imply a human mind, imply cognition, imply reason. But the notion that humor, per se, does not exist, that it is all a matter of someone's opinion, is very problematical.

Just because John Q. Public does not laugh at joke X does not mean joke X is not funny. He may not get the joke or it may be on a subject he does not consider appropriate for jokes. But it is very difficult to argue that humor (like beauty) exists merely in the eye of the beholder. If humor or beauty or anything is merely a matter of someone's opinion, everything dissolves in the acid of particularism and one is left with a solipsistic perspective on things. Everyone is entitled to his or her taste or sense of humor, I would suggest, but that does not mean that his or her taste or sense of humor is all that counts.

This argument can be stated in terms of a dispute found in literary criticism. Is what critics find in a text a matter of "God's truth" (discovering interesting things hidden in the text) or "hocus-pocus" (reading things into the text that are not there)? Are there jokes, cartoons, and plays that are humorous or is it all a matter of opinion, and does what we call humor always involve an individual "reading" humor, so to speak, into these jokes, cartoons, and plays? If it is essentially reading in, the question I asked earlier must be answered: How do we explain the fact that large numbers of people laugh at the same time when they are watching a "humorous" play or movie or listening to a comedian? I don't believe that humor exists only in the mind of the laugher, but that it exists in the real world.

Humor About Philosophers

Philosophers are themselves frequently the subjects of jokes and of much humor, in part, because of the somewhat esoteric nature of their concerns—ones that are often couched in highly technical terms and are often far removed from the knowledge base of most people.

In this respect, consider an early work, Samuel Butler's poem *Hudibras*, the first part of which was written in 1663. In this poem we find a comic description of a person who has many different talents—he is a philosopher, a rhetorician, and so on. In his philosophic mode he is described as follows:

> *He was in Logic a great critic,*
> *Profoundly skill'd in Analytic.*
> *He could distinguish, and divide*
> *A hair 'twixt south and south-west side;*
> *On either which he would dispute,*
> *Confute, change hands, and still confute.*
> *He'd undertake to prove, by force*
> *Of argument, a man's no horse.*
> *He'd prove a buzzard is no fowl,*
> *And that a Lord may be an owl,*
> *A calf an Alderman, a goose a Justice,*
> *And rooks, Committee-men and Trustees;*

He'd run in debt by disputation,
And pay with ratiocination.
All this by syllogism true,
In mood and figure, he would do.

The hero of this poem is shown to be a somewhat unworldly pedant, who uses his intellect for various absurd reasons that make him an object of ridicule. He could make extremely fine distinctions but they led to nothing, for this "brilliant" thinker spent his intellectual energy in proving a man's not a horse and that a Lord may be an owl. This is tied to the stereotype we have of philosophers as people with considerable intellect but who tend to be unworldly and without much common sense. It is his perverse use of logic that is made fun of here. He abuses logic— like many philosophers (and ordinary people as well, as Ionesco's characters in *The Bald Soprano* demonstrate).

Woody Allen has made fun of philosophy in "Spring Bulletin," a parody of college bulletin course descriptions that appeared in *The New Yorker* (29 April 1967):

> Philosophy I: *Everyone from Plato to Camus is read and the following topics are covered: Ethics: The categorical imperative and six ways to make it work for you. Aesthetics: Is art the mirror of life, or what? Metaphysics: What happens to the soul after death? How does it manage? Epistemology: Is knowledge knowable? If not, how do we know this? The Absurd: Why existence is often considered silly, particularly for men who wear brown and white shoes. Manyness and Oneness are studied as they relate to otherness. (Students achieving oneness will move ahead to twoness.)*

Allen's essay is a parody of the prose styles found in college bulletins, but parodies, we must remember, generally use other techniques of humor besides imitation to amuse readers. In this essay, in addition to spoofing philosophy, we find a parody of advertising techniques (six ways to make the categorical imperative work for you). We also find absurdity (existence is silly for men with brown and white shoes), ridicule (how do we know if knowledge is not knowable?), and wordplay (oneness and twoness). These techniques, and others as well, are dealt with in the chapter that follows on rhetorical approaches to humor.

Conclusions

Philosophers have been interested in humor throughout history, from Plato and Aristotle to the present day. Hobbes's theory, which argues that humor is tied to a sense of superiority, provides an important insight into the relationship between those who laugh and those who are the objects of laughter. And Bergson offers us an example of a theory of humor—which states that humor involves "the mechanical encrusted on the living"—that can be logically extended to cover a large number of different kinds of humor. It may be somewhat reductionistic, but it is remarkable how it can be used to explain humor of situation, personality, and so on. The existentialist notion that humor is tied to the absurd and that life is, to a great degree, absurd was also discussed.

Bergson, Kant, and Schopenhauer have all elaborated on what we might describe as an "incongruity" theory of humor, which suggests that all humor is connected to some difference between what we expect and what we get—whether in the punch line of a joke or in the actions of comic characters. The question of the ontological status of humor— whether it actually exists or is merely something in the mind of the laugher—is discussed, and it is suggested that saying humor exists only in the mind is reductionistic and ultimately solipsistic.

Finally, some examples of humor about philosophers are offered— by Samuel Butler and Woody Allen. Philosophers are good targets for humorists since philosophical concerns seem esoteric and very technical (ivory towerish) and far removed from the everyday concerns of most people, though, in actuality, this is not the case.

References

Allen, Woody. "Spring Bulletin." *The New Yorker.* 29 April 1967.
Chapman, Tony, and Hugh Foot, eds. *Humour and Laughter: Theory, Research and Applications.* London: John Wiley & Sons, 1976.
Hobbes, Thomas. *Leviathan.* Oxford: Basil Blackwell, 1957.
Koestler, Arthur. *Insight and Outlook.* New York: MacMillan, 1949.
McKeon, Richard, ed. *The Basic Works of Aristotle.* New York: Random House, 1941.
Piddington, Ralph. *The Psychology of Laughter.* New York: Gamut Press, 1963.
Sypher, Wylie, ed. *Comedy.* Garden City, NY: Anchor Books, 1956.

A glance at some of the common features of comic lines, behavior or situations reveals a close analogy between comic techniques and Zen techniques, as well as the serviceability of comic techniques in Zen: irrationality, contradiction, incongruity, absurdity, irrelevancy, triviality, nonsense, distortion, abruptness, shock, sudden twist, reversal or overturning. In both comedy and Zen one is prevented from drawing a purely intellectual conclusion at the end of an argument and therefore entering the abstractness and deceptiveness of a pseudo-appropriation of truth.

—Conrad Hyers
Zen and the Comic Spirit

4

The Rhetoric of Laughter:
The Techniques Used in Humor

Technically speaking, rhetoric is the art of persuasion, though contemporary rhetoricians often use the term much more broadly. Aristotle defined the term rather narrowly (by today's standards) in his book the *Rhetoric*:

> Rhetoric may be defined as the faculty of observing in any given case the available means of persuasion. This is not a function of any other art. Every other art can instruct or persuade about its own particular subject-matter....But rhetoric we look upon as the power of observing the means of persuasion on almost any subject presented to us; and that is why we say that, in its technical character, it is not concerned with any special or definite class of subjects. (1941, 1329)

Rhetoric, for Aristotle, is a metadiscipline, one that can be used to analyze how people persuade others regardless of subject matter or content.

Aristotle adds that there are three basic modes of persuasion in speeches (and we could add other written forms, as well): the first is based on the character and reputation of the speaker; the second is based on putting the audience into an emotional state in which it is most susceptible to persuasion; and the third is based on the proof, or apparent proof, provided by the speech—that is, the logical aspects of the argument made by the speaker, or writer.

This focus on persuasion no longer dominates rhetorical studies, which have moved from a concern (or perhaps preoccupation would be a better term) with argumentation, debate, and related matters to other areas. Rhetoricians also concern themselves nowadays with topics such as how written communication works, with the nature of narrativity in works of fiction and films and with stylistics in general.

Rhetoric has been used to analyze popular culture and interpret television and televised texts. For example, there are books such as Robert L. Root, Jr.'s *The Rhetoric of Popular Culture,* Ronald Primeau's *The*

Rhetoric of Television, and Martin J. Medhurst and Thomas W. Benson's *Rhetorical Dimensions in Media: A Critical Casebook.* These books, and others like them, use concepts taken from rhetorical analysis to deal with popular culture and television. Primeau offers his understanding of rhetoric. Explaining that the term *rhetoric* comes from *rhetor* or "orator" he suggests that rhetoric:

> attempts to explain how human beings invent, arrange, and present ideas and feelings. The communication model developed in classical rhetoric was an attempt to describe systematically the complex techniques human beings use first to create and then to communicate those creations and finally to respond to the creations of others. (1979, 21)

Primeau describes the classical model.

It is based on five processes:

1. *inventio* or inventing or creating messages, texts, etc.
2. *dispositio* or arranging or organizing into parts what had been invented or created.
3. *elocutio* or the stylistic aspects of the message.
4. *pronunciato* or delivering the message to an audience via some medium.
5. *memoria* or techniques used by message inventors to make memorable what they had created, arranged, stylized and delivered, such as alliteration, repetition, use of figurative language, and so forth. (1979, 21)

These processes can be found in all communication and Primeau's book involves helping students to use them to analyze everything from television commercials to documentaries.

Medhurst and Benson discuss the different interpretations of rhetoric and offer a list of nine views of how rhetoric can be used. These "senses" of rhetoric are not, they point out, mutually exclusive. These (1984, xx, xxi) are:

1. Rhetoric as intentional persuasion.
2. Rhetoric as the social values and effects of symbolic forms, whether intentional or not.
3. Rhetoric as the techniques by which nondidactic arts communicate to audiences.
4. Rhetoric as the persuasion addressed by one character to another within a dramatic or narrative work.
5. Rhetoric as the body of principles and techniques of rhetorical theory—the traditional resources of invention, disposition, style, memory, and delivery as they are discovered in texts.

6. Rhetoric as the study of genres or types.
7. Implicit rhetorical theory: rhetoric as theories about human symbolic interaction implied by the authors of symbolic forms.
8. Rhetoric as an ideal for the conduct of human communication.
9. Rhetoric as the study of what gives effectiveness to form; the pragmatics of human communication.

This list casts rhetoric in a much broader perspective than the Aristotelian one and uses rhetorical principles to analyze texts carried by the mass media.

A Modification to Analyze Humor

My analysis of humor from a rhetorical perspective involves using rhetoric in this broad sense of the subject, but I think you will see that there is also a connection between the methodology I will be elaborating and traditional rhetoric. My concern is not with techniques that can be used to persuade people to believe something but techniques that can be used to "persuade" people to laugh or, at the least, to see or define some text or performance as humorous. My focus is on techniques or what classical rhetoricians called *memoria* in Primeau's typology or items three and four in the list offered above.

A number of years ago, after reading numerous works by philosophers and others, I decided that I could not find a satisfactory explanation for why people laugh. So I decided to try to answer a different question: What is it that makes people laugh? The focus of this second question was on techniques used by humorists of all kinds to generate humor and laughter. I made an elaborate content analysis of everything in my library that was humorous: joke books, comic books, plays, novels, cartoons, comic essays, and so on. I discovered that the subject of a joke often was not important; I'd see the same joke told about a general in one joke book and a politician in another joke book.

I concluded then that subject matter was of secondary importance and that it was the techniques used by humorists that were of central importance. As a result of my labors I was able to come up with forty-five techniques that writers, artists, stand-up comedians, and so forth, use or have used to generate laughter or create humor. I was not able to find other techniques, though some may have eluded me. A given technique often can be reversed or used in different ways, I might add. Thus, insults, an important technique, can be turned against oneself and become victim humor. I listed insults as the technique, recognizing that it could be reversed or directed in varying ways. The same kind of thing can be done with another important technique, exaggeration. When reversed it becomes understatement.

I also found that my list of forty-five techniques could be broken down into four categories: humor involving identity, humor involving logic, humor involving language, and humor involving sight or action—what I call visual humor. I wanted to have a way of dealing with sight gags, chase scenes in comic films, and that kind of thing and have a few techniques to deal with these matters.

My list of the forty-five techniques follows. I will list the technique and then put the category in parentheses.

1.	Absurdity	(logic)
2.	Accident	(logic)
3.	Allusion	(language)
4.	Analogy	(logic)
5.	Before/After	(identity)
6.	Bombast	(language)
7.	Burlesque	(identity)
8.	Caricature	(identity)
9.	Catalogue	(logic)
10.	Chase scene	(visual)
11.	Coincidence	(logic)
12.	Comparison	(logic)
13.	Definition	(language)
14.	Disappointment	(logic)
15.	Eccentricity	(identity)
16.	Embarrassment	(identity)
17.	Exaggeration	(language)
18.	Exposure	(identity)
19.	Facetiousness	(language)
20.	Grotesque	(identity)
21.	Ignorance	(logic)
22.	Imitation	(identity)
23.	Impersonation	(identity)
24.	Infantilism	(language)
25.	Insults	(language)

26.	Irony	(language)
27.	Literalness	(language)
28.	Mimicry	(identity)
29.	Mistakes	(logic)
30.	Misunderstanding	(language)
31.	Parody	(identity)
32.	Puns, Wordplay	(language)
33.	Repartee, Outwitting	(language)
34.	Repetition, Pattern	(logic)
35.	Reversal	(logic)
36.	Ridicule	(language)
37.	Rigidity	(logic)
38.	Sarcasm	(language)
39.	Satire	(language)
40.	Scale, Size	(identity)
41.	Slapstick	(visual)
42.	Speed	(visual)
43.	Stereotypes	(identity)
44.	Theme and Variation	(logic)
45.	Unmasking	(identity)

Basic Techniques of Humor Generation

These techniques can be used to deconstruct, so to speak, any example of humor, whether it is a scene from a play by Molière, Aristophanes, Shakespeare, or Neil Simon, or a cartoon, or a joke, or whatever. That is, I believe that my list of techniques enables us to see how writers, comedians, film makers, stand-up comics, and so on, create humorous material—and these techniques, I would add, have been used from the earliest comedies until the present day.

There is a problem with some of my techniques. Some are very broad, such as satire and parody, and others are rather narrow, such as insult. I have lumped together genres, styles, and other methods and this might disturb some (might we describe them as purists?) who feel my list confuses categories too much. But the list has one very important quality: it does enable us to see how jokes and other examples of humor work, so despite its limitations, I think my list of techniques is a useful contribution to understanding humor. There is no other typology that I know of

that enables us to understand the mechanisms or techniques that generate humor in any text with such a high degree of specificity.

Let me now use my list of techniques to analyze some texts. I should
point out that we often find a number of techniques at work in a text,
though usually one technique is dominant.

Humorous Definition

I will start with a relatively simple text, a humorous definition:

A behaviorist is someone who pulls habits out of rats.

This is not a joke (that is, a story with a punchline) but a comic definition,
one that is meant to be amusing. However, humor of definition is not all
there is in this text. There is an element of ridicule (of behaviorists, who
are made fun of by this comic definition). In addition, there is allusion and
reversal, for unlike the magician, who pulls rabbits out of hats, the behaviorist pulls habits out of rats. Pulling habits out of rats doesn't mean anything, doesn't have a comic aspect to it, unless one has heard of and perhaps
seen magicians pulling rabbits out of hats. The reversal involves switch-
ing the letters *r* and *h* from rabbits to habits and from hat to rat. You can
see, then, that even a relatively simple text may be quite complicated in
terms of the techniques used in it to generate humor.

Humor Involving Mistakes

*There are two friends, one is white and the other is an African-American. One
evening they get into an argument about which one of them can have sex the most
times in one night. So they go to a local whore house, pair off with their partners,
and go to their rooms. The white man has sex with his partner, puts a 1 on the wall
and falls asleep. A few hours later he wakes up again, has sex with his partner, puts
another 1 on the wall and falls back asleep. He sets his alarm and they get up early
in the morning. When they get up he has sex again and once again puts a 1 on the
wall. A short while after, the African-American knocks on the white guy's door and
enters the room. He takes a look at the wall and says, "A hundred and eleven! You
beat me by three."*

There are a number of techniques used in this joke. First, the punch line
is based on a mistake, so we could argue that the dominant technique in
the joke is mistakes. A mistake is some kind of an error we make, something we do that is wrong. It differs from misunderstanding, which involves incorrectly interpreting something that is said.

The African-American sees the three marks and interprets them as one-hundred and eleven instead of three. But he does this because he has had sex one-hundred and eight times that evening. The sexual heroics of the African-American involves two techniques: stereotyping of African-Americans as being sexual supermen (and, as such objects, of fear and anxiety by white males who cannot compete with them) and gross exaggeration. The white man has barely managed to have sex three times and the African-American has had sex one-hundred and eight times. There is also comic comparison at work, which is another important technique of humor.

Insult Humor

Here, I will quote from Shakespeare's *Henry the Fourth*, Part I, a scene in which Prince Hal and Falstaff insult one another:

> PRINCE. *I'll be no longer guilty of this sin. This sanguine coward, this bed presser, this horseback-breaker, this huge hill of flesh—*
>
> FALSTAFF. *'Sblood, you starveling, you eel-skin, you dried neat's-tongue, you bull's pizzle, you stockfish. O for breath to utter what is like thee! You tailor's yard, you sheath, you bowcase, you vile standing tuck!* (Act 2, scene 4)

Hal is describing how lazy and fat Falstaff is, suggesting he spends most of his time in bed (a bed presser) and is so fat that he breaks the backs of horses. Falstaff counters by suggesting that Prince Hal is extremely thin, like an eelskin, a dried codfish, a yardstick, or a rapier.

These insults are not meaningful to us today, but they were to Shakespeare's audiences. We now have other kinds of insults we make, and some humorists, such as Don Rickles and Andrew Dice Clay, use insults as the basis of their humor. But insult humor is always dangerous, because the aggression expressed in insults often is not considered humorous by the person or persons who are insulted.

Personal Style and Humor

My list of techniques enables us to see what is distinctive in a humorist and better defines what might be called a humorist's voice or style. Humorists establish an identity for themselves, based in part on the subjects they deal with but mostly based on the techniques they tend to use most often in their work. Consider, for example, Woody Allen's literary efforts—the stories he writes for *The New Yorker*. Let me offer a quotation that I believe is representative of his work—taken from his story "My Philosophy" (Allen, 1978). His story starts as follows:

> *The development of my philosophy came about as follows: My wife, inviting me to sample her very first souffle, accidentally dropped a spoonful of it on my foot, fracturing several small bones. Doctors were called in, X-rays taken and examined, and I was ordered to bed for a month. During this convalescence, I turned to the works of some of Western society's most formidable thinkers—a stack of books I had laid aside for just such an occasion. Scorning chronological order, I began with Kierkegaard and Sartre, then moved quickly to Spinoza, Hume, Kafka, and Camus. I was not bored, as I had feared I might be; rather, I found myself fascinated by the alacrity with which these great minds unflinchingly attacked morality, art, ethics, life, and death. I remember my reaction to a typically luminous observation of Kierkegaard's: "Such a relation which relates itself to its own self (that is to say, a self) must either have constituted itself or have been constituted by another." The concept brought tears to my eyes. My word, to be that clever! (I'm a man who has trouble writing two meaningful sentences on "My Day at the Zoo.")*

In this passage we see that Allen is dealing with one of his favorite subjects: intellectuals (and often neurotic Jewish intellectuals). Some of his other characters have names such as Hans Metterling and Rabbi Ben Kaddish, as well as famous personalities with whom they interact such as Gertrude Stein, Picasso, Hemingway, and Matisse.

He mentions a number of important modern philosophers and then makes fun of them by quoting something from Kierkegaard that is just about unintelligible. But his hero, a victim of his wife's souffle, a spoonful of which was enough to break some bones in his foot, is awed by these great thinkers and decides, in fact, to become a metaphysician and leaves a sampling of his work for posterity, or until the cleaning woman arrives. Allen often uses this device of citing something seemingly serious or important, such as his philosophical works that are left for posterity, and following it up with something that belittles or makes fun of the original concept, such as the cleaning lady. In the same light, he discusses the works of great philosophers and then mentions that he'd have trouble writing two sentences about some mundane subject, such as his visit to the zoo. This technique is at work in the mock aphorism with which he ends his story: "Not only is there no God, but try getting a plumber on weekends." Here we have the same phenomenon—a seemingly momentous statement about there not being a God followed by the trivial statement about how difficult it is to get a plumber on weekends.

The philosophical fragments our hero leaves behind are parodies of traditional philosophical writing, and it is parody that I would suggest is one of Allen's central techniques. His stories are generally parodies on the most common formulaic texts that educated and "sophisticated" elements are exposed to or would know about—descriptions of ballets, fragments of the Dead Sea Scrolls, private-eye tough-guy detectives, classical detectives, literary criticism, bestiaries (of magic animals), Socratic dialogues, and so on. In his parodies, Allen uses his technique of tying the momentous to the trivial and links nobodies with great writers and artists.

He does so with great wit and imagination and has peopled his stories with a group of really weird characters—the technique I describe as eccentricity. His characters tend to be hyperintellectual, raunchy, neurotic, urban types such as Professor Kugelmass, a professor of humanities at City College, Moses Goldworm, and Fabian Plotnick, the high-minded restaurant critic whose review of Fabrizio's Villa Nova restaurant generated a number of heated responses. This piece, "Fabrizio's: Criticism and Response" starts as follows:

> Pasta as an expression of Italian Neo-Realistic starch is well understood by Mario Spinelli, the chef at Fabrizio's. Spinelli kneads his pasta slowly. He allows a buildup of tension by the customers as they sit salivating. His fettucine, through wry and puckish in an almost mischievous way, owes a lot to Barzino, whose use of fettucine as an instrument of social change is known to us all. (Allen, 1981)

Here Allen is parodying the high seriousness of many restaurant critics—the way they use language, the sense they have that food is of central importance in the scheme of things, and things like that. We see such restaurant reviews in *The New York Times, Gourmet,* and other such publications, typically read by upper-middle-class intellectuals. The combination of extreme elements here involves using high seriousness and lofty philosophical concerns (neorealism, social change) to deal with pasta, something very common and ordinary.

Samuel Butler Makes Fun of Rhetoric

In *Hudibras, Part I,* a mock heroic written in 1663, Samuel Butler satirizes English Puritans, and in doing so, makes fun of rhetoric (as well as many other things, I might add). In it he ridicules rhetoricians as follows:

> *For Rhetoric, he could not ope*
> *His mouth but out there flew a trope:*
> *And when he happen'd to break off*
> *I' th' middle of his speech, or cough,*
> *H' had hard words ready to show why,*
> *And tell what rules he did it by.*
> *Else, when with greatest art he spoke,*
> *You'd think he talk'd like other folk,*
> *For all a rhetorician's rules*
> *Teach nothing but to name his tools.*

Butler's satire on rhetoric continues on a good deal longer, but this gives you a sense of what he wrote. It also shows that rhetoricians have been the objects of people's attention, and in some cases ridicule, for more than 300 years. Since Aristotle wrote on rhetoric, we can see that this science has been with us for a great deal of time. Butler used an octosyllabic couplet and wrote in iambic tetrameter, in which the couplets rhyme as follows: *aa-bb* and so on.

Hudibras is famous for its brilliant and often shocking rhymes (sometimes double and even triple rhymes) as well as its satire on the Puritans; verse written in its style is even called Hudibrastic verse.

Conclusions

A rhetorical approach to humorous texts, as I use the term and as many contemporary rhetoricians understand their subject, involves understanding the techniques used by writers, artists, film makers, and others to generate humor. A list of forty-five techniques found in humor was offered and applied to a variety of texts: jokes, dialogue in a play by Shakespeare, and humorous short stories by Woody Allen. I have suggested, also, that the techniques a humorist typically uses can be isolated and help us understand his or her style or what might be described as an authorial (that is, distinctive to a writer or creator of humorous texts, regardless of medium) "voice."

References

Allen, Woody. *Getting Even*. New York: Vantage, 1978.
———. *Side Effects*. New York: Ballantine, 1981.
Medhurst, Martin J., and Thomas W. Benson, eds. *Rhetorical Dimensions in Media: A Critical Casebook*. Dubuque, Iowa: Kendall/Hunt, 1984.

Primeau, Ronald. *The Rhetoric of Television.* New York: Longman, 1979.
Shakespeare, William. *Henry the Fourth,* Part I. James L. Sanderson, ed. New York: Norton, 1962.

My hypothesis is that a joke is seen and allowed when it offers a symbolic pattern of a social pattern occurring at the same time. As I see it, all jokes are expressive of social situations in which they occur. The one social condition necessary for a joke to be employed is that the social group in which it is received should develop the formal characteristics of a "told" joke: that is, a dominant pattern of relations is challenged by another. If there is no joke in the social structure, no other joking can occur.

—Mary Douglas
"Jokes." *Implicit Meanings*

5

The Structure of Laughter:
Semiotics and Humor

Semiotics, the science of signs, has some interesting insights to offer about humor. In this chapter I discuss some of the more important semiotic concepts and use them to analyze humorous texts. I consider such things as the structure of jokes, the relation of humor to code violations, and the various kinds of parody that exist.

A sign, the semioticians tell us, is anything that can be used to stand for or substitute for something else. What semiotics concerns itself with, in essence, is how meaning is produced. In linguistic parlance, at the most elementary level of analysis, we have senders who create texts that are decoded by addressees, those who receive the texts.

Humor as Code Violations

Saussure, one of the founding fathers of the science of signs (he called his version of it semiology), reminds us that signs are made up of two parts: a sound image or signifier and a concept or signified. The relation between the signifier and signified is arbitrary, a matter of convention, which means that we all have to learn what signs mean. In essence, we learn a number of codes, which can be thought of as rules that tell us how to interpret signs. Saussure called his science of signs *semiology* in contrast to C. S. Peirce, another important theorist of signs, who called his science *semiotics*. He argued that there are three kinds of signs: icons, which signify by resemblance; indexes, which signify by cause and effect; and symbols, whose meaning must be learned. The term *semiotics* is the one most commonly used now for the study of signs and I will use the term for either perspective on signs.

From a semiotic point of view, humor can be thought of as involving some kind of a code violation. This notion can be thought of as a semiotic variation on the concept of incongruity. According to this incongruity theory, humor is based on some kind of a surprise, in which what you get is not what you might anticipate. In jokes, when you reach the punch line there is a resolution of the story that is surprising and it is this unexpected resolution that generates the laughter. Logic would dictate that a text should end in a certain way that is tied, somehow, to the events told in the text. But in joke texts, punch lines always confound us and offer resolutions of situations (created in the narrative of the joke) that are unanticipated. Jokes, let us remember, are stories meant to amuse that have punch lines.

In an article "Jokes as Text Types" in *Humor* (vol. 5, no. 1/2, 1992), Salvatore Attardo and Jean-Charles Chabanne argue that jokes satisfy the requirements that various semioticians have elaborated to qualify as texts. They define jokes as follows (1992, 172):

> [A] joke is an anonymous, partially or completely recycled text that contains a non-bona fide linguistic/cognitive disturbance (the punch line) that "closes" the previous text. The text itself is tendentially short and contains the basic features of a narrative.

They consider jokes to be "micro-narratives" that contain all the features of texts, along with the necessary punch lines.

This "punch line" is also found in other kinds of humorous texts, such as comic poetry. For example, consider the following poem:

ON A POLITICIAN

Here, richly, with ridiculous display,
The Politician's corpse was laid away.
While all of his acquaintance sneered and slanged,
I wept: for I had longed to see him hanged.
                              —Hilaire Belloc

The last line, here, about the man weeping turns into a surprise: he was weeping not because he is sad about the man's death but because the politician had died a natural death and escaped what he really deserved—according to the weeping man—hanging.

The notion of humor as a kind of code violation is also close to Bergson's view that humor involves the mechanical encrusted on the living. Comedy, as has been pointed out, is often based on bizarre types—

characters who are monomaniacs, fixated on one particular passion, dominated by a humor: some are misers, some are hypochondriacs, some are boasters, and so on. This, we can say, represents a violation of the code that humans are supposed to be reasonable individuals, that we should be flexible and fit in with others, not cause all kinds of complications by being so one-dimensional, so rigid. The following joke deals with rigidity and uses it as a source of amusement:

> *A man is at his club and notices an elderly gentlemen who seems ill at ease. The man decides to see whether he can be of assistance. "Would you be interested in playing a game of cards?" he asks the old man. "No," says the old man. "Tried it once and didn't like it." The man then says, "Would you like to play some billiards?" "No," says the old man. "Tried it once and didn't like it!" The man decides to make one last try. "Can I get you a drink?" he asks. "No," says the old man. "Tried it once and didn't like it! Besides, my son will be coming to get me soon." "Your only son, I imagine!" replies the man.*

Here, the rigidity of the old man, who has tried various things once and didn't like them, is turned into something comic. It is suggested that, like everything else, he probably tried sex only once and "didn't like it" either.

The Narrative Structure and Ideational Content of Jokes

I am using jokes here because they are relatively simple to deal with, but they aren't different in nature, we may say, from other kinds of humor—except that jokes have punch lines while other kinds of humor may be based on insult, satire, parody, and so on. Semioticians distinguish between the syntagmatic and paradigmatic analysis of texts. The syntagmatic perspective looks at the narrative structure of the text; how it proceeds from one event to the next. A syntagm is a chain. The paradigmatic perspective, as I will use the term, examines texts in terms of the pattern of oppositions in the text that give it meaning. A paradigmatic analysis, we might say, is based on taking Saussure's notion that concepts are defined differentially and applying it to texts.

A syntagmatic analysis of the joke about the old man would go as follows:

$$A \rightarrow B \rightarrow C \rightarrow D \rightarrow E \rightarrow F \text{ (syntagmatic)}$$
$$\downarrow$$
$$G \text{ (paradigmatic)}$$

A through E represent the various parts of the joke and F represents the punch line, where the club member says "your only son." This generates the laughter and establishes G, the paradigmatic meaning of the text, the basic opposition: rigid versus flexible. Other oppositions implied in the joke are things such as: open to experience versus closed to experience, hedonistic versus ascetic, friendly versus distant, and so on.

I should point out that in a joke we usually find a number of different humorous techniques at play. This joke is based on rigidity but it also involves repartee (a good comeback to the "tried it once and didn't like it" response of the old man) and, perhaps, sarcasm (the punch line is somewhat snide).

It is also conceivable that there is a structural correspondence between signs and punch lines. The relation between a signifier and a signified is conventional (not natural, not fixed, not based on logic) and the relation between the events in a joke and the punch line is also not natural or logical. It is that very relationship, the fact that the punch line cannot be inferred from the events in the joke that precede it, that allows the punch line to generate laughter. The chart that follows shows this visually:

SIGN	JOKE
Signifier/Signified	Events in joke before punch line
Arbitrary relationship	*Unanticipated resolution*
Meaning	Punch line and laughter

Perhaps the arbitrary nature of the sign has something to do with the unanticipated resolution generated by the punch line—a resolution that causes laughter.

Puns: Not the Lowest Form of Wit

Puns are often attacked as being "the lowest form of wit." This is not true; good puns are excellent examples of wit. It is only when the pun stretches too far or is too far off base that puns elicit the customary groan from people—a response we all learn as proper when dealing with a pun that doesn't work.

From a semiotic perspective, a pun is an auditory signifier that has two signifieds. Let me offer an example and explain it in semiotic terms:

An English wit couldn't help himself but made puns on all occasions. On being taken to see an orphanage he said "this far and no father." The next morning, he declared, biting into a roll, "the bun is the lowest form of wheat."

The first pun involves a play on the phrase "no father." The phrase means either of two things: no farther (in terms of distance) or no father (in terms of being orphans). The second pun plays on the notion that the "pun is the lowest form of wit" and substitutes "bun" for "pun" and uses it to stand for "wheat," which is a play on words with the term "wit." Let me diagram the first pun below.

Signifier: Orphan Asylum

↙   ↘

Signified 1: No farther (distance) *Signified* 2: No father (orphan)

Diagram of Pun and Signifier/Signified Relationship

The difference between a good pun and a poor pun is now evident. A good pun involves a play on sound as well as a play on meaning, while a poor pun essentially involves a play on sound.

Metaphor and Humor of Analogy

Metaphor is a literary device that relates two things by analogy. "My love is a rose" is a metaphor; the two parts of the metaphor are equated: my love and a rose. As such, it is a stronger form of analogy than a simile, which uses "like" or "as" to soften the connection. "My love is *like* a rose" is a simile; you can see that it isn't as powerful a figure as a metaphor.

Metaphors and similes are often used to create humor. For example, one of the more common techniques of humor involves insult, and it is relatively easy to insult a person using metaphors and similes. If we were to say about someone, "He's a big jackass," we are offering an insulting metaphor, equating the person with a jackass (a dumb beast with a reputation for being ornery). When we call people names, we are using metaphor:

He's a nerd.

She's a yuppie.

He's a creep.

He's an asshole.

All of these terms are ones that poke fun (or worse) at people and terms that we use to put people down, since we identify them with types of people who are often ridiculed or parts of the body that are not considered beautiful or nice.

When I was in the army there was a vulgar riddle that people used to amuse themselves with that was metaphoric in structure.

> *Question:*   *Name two things that look the same.*
>
> *Answer:*   *Your face and my ass.*

That is, the joke asserts, "Your face is like my ass." I would describe this riddle as very high on aggressive content and quite low on comic value.

Metonymy

Metonymy is a figure of speech that uses association to generate meaning. For an example of metonymy, imagine a large mansion. Large mansions tend to be associated with great wealth in people's minds—in part because it costs a great deal of money to build a large mansion and because of the expense of running it: keeping it clean, paying for the fuel to keep it warm or cool, and so on.

Synecdoche is a weaker form of metonymy. In synecdoche, a part can be used to stand for a whole, or vice versa. It seems likely that synecdoche is the mechanism that is basic to stereotyping, one of the most important techniques of humor. A stereotype is a generalization about some group of people (Jews, African-Americans, Scots, Englishmen, Southerners, WASPs, etc.) based on acquaintance with a relatively limited number of people from the group. What we think of *some*, we apply to *all*.

Consider the following joke about Jewish American Princesses or JAPS. Actually the JAP jokes are technically riddles, in which a question is asked and then the answer is given:

> *Question:*   *How do you tickle a JAP?*
>
> *Answer:*   *Gucci, Gucci, cooh.*

I've seen this joke also told about Nancy Reagan, as a matter of fact, so it isn't limited to JAPS. But Nancy Reagan is known as a person overly concerned with fashion, so it is understandable why the joke might be applied to her. The stereotype here is that JAPS are materialistic, overly fashion conscious, and like expensive clothes. Hence, the use of "Gucci" instead of "coochy."

A Note on Clowns

Clowns are comic figures found in circuses and other similar entertainments such as ice shows and carnivals. The very look of clowns, with their exaggerated makeup (red bulbous noses, etc.) and their costumes (baggy pants, tiny derbies, big feet, etc.) announces that they are comic figures. We wouldn't necessarily interpret these phenomena as funny on our own, but after seeing one or two clowns horsing around we recognize that a clown is, semiotically speaking, a system of exaggerated signs. All of these signs suggest, by their exaggerated nature, that we are seeing characters who look funny and will act funny.

Clowns engage in exaggerated behavior to match their costumes: they hit each other over the head with huge mallets, they trip over things and tumble around, and they have objects that make funny noises or are absurd. The humor is very broad and often full of physical activity and slapstick. In this respect they take ordinary behavior—certain facial expressions we make, our body language, speech patterns, dialects, and absurd logic that we sometimes follow—and blow it up to ridiculous proportions. Clowns, then, take signs and push them to their extreme limits. The physical humor of clowns, let me add, can be analyzed using the forty-five techniques I elaborated on earlier in my chapter on rhetorical approaches to humor. These techniques deal with physical humor, verbal humor, and, as we will see later, with visual humor as well.

In an essay "A Semiotic Approach to Nonsense: Clowns and Limericks," Paul Bouissac discusses limericks and clowns. After expressing a sense of bewilderment about the existence of limericks, he moves on to clowns and writes (Bouissac, 1978, 244–45):

> The existence of clowns is equally puzzling; their performances comprise manipulation of special artifacts, stereotyped "illogical" behavior, distinctive garments and make-up, and dialogues that are spoken or mimed. Their tradition is transmitted mainly through observational learning, either in a family context or by individual apprenticeship, or even in official institutions such as the Clown College set up by Ringling Brothers Barnum and Bailey Circus in Venice, Florida, or the State School for circus performers in the Soviet Union.

The outcome of all this training is the basic routine of clowns, which Bouissac suggests involves "apparently inadequate conduct, intellectual or physical shortcomings, impossible situations, and irrational artifacts" (Bouissac, 1978, 245).

What is important to recognize about clowns (and limericks as well), as Bouissac points out, is that performances by clowns (and those who make limericks) are not haphazard by any means, but are governed strictly by rules. These rules, he suggests, are not rigidly formalized but we recognize that they are lacking when we see a poor performance by clowns. In this respect he describes a clown act performed by two French clowns—a white clown (with white makeup) and another clown who continually interrupts and disrupts the white clown. The white clown is elegant and articulate but the other clown is just the opposite: he has an awkward gait, he wears crazy clothes and makeup, and engages in nonsensical behavior.

These two clowns can be seen, Bouissac suggests, as embodiments of the opposition between culture and nature—one of the primary oppositions that we make. His reasoning that leads to this conclusion is too lengthy to be dealt with here, but the fact that these clowns do stand for a set of basic polar oppositions is important.

What is significant about clowns, Bouissac concludes, is that ultimately they deal with very sensitive matters, they touch upon taboo topics, and they manipulate "delicate logical constructs that are the very foundations of our sense of rational reality" (Bouissac, 1978, 256). Thus, though clowns engage in certain kinds of behaviors that seem relatively simple and crude, in reality what clowns do is much more complicated than we recognize and clowns pose difficult problems for semioticians who want to decode their actions and understand how and what they signify.

Parody and Intertextuality

Intertextuality occurs when a text makes reference to another text. As Neal R. Norrick defines it in his essay "Intertextuality in Humor":

Intertextuality occurs any time one text suggests or requires reference to some other identifiable text or stretch of discourse, spoken or written. Scholarly writing seems to make its intertextual references as accurate and conspicuous as possible through documentation, while everyday conversation borrows freely from sources

often left unnamed, and literature delights in disguise, obscure allusion, and parody.
(1989, 117-18)

Parody is often cited as one of the most frequently used examples of
intertextuality. Parody relies on the addressee recognizing the original
text in order to get the most out of the humor, though in some parodies
the exaggeration and absurdity of the text itself is enough to please
audiences.

I think of parody as a technique of humor that is based on the category of humor of identity. I suggest there are three kinds of parody:
ridiculing a style of authorship (including visual arts), a genre (such as a
soap opera), or a specific text (such as *Star Wars*). Let me offer some
examples, with the caveat that in some cases, genres have a particular
style so the separation between genre and style is not always easy to
make. In addition to ridiculous imitation, parodies often use other techniques of humor such as exaggeration, definition, and absurdity.

Parody of Style

In "Spring Bulletin," referred to in chapter 3, Woody Allen parodies
the style of writing found in college bulletins:

INTRODUCTION TO PSYCHOLOGY

*The theory of human behavior. Why some men are called "lovely individuals" and
why there are others you just want to pinch. Is there a split between mind and body,
and, if so, which is better to have? Aggression and rebellion are discussed. (Students particularly interested in these aspects of psychology are advised to take one
of the Winter Term courses: Introduction to Hostility; Intermediate Hostility; Ad-
vanced Hatred; Theoretical Foundations of Loathing.) Special consideration is
given to a study of consciousness as opposed to unconsciousness, with many help-
ful hints on how to remain conscious.*

Allen, who claims never to have read anything except comic books in
his formative years, offers a real send-up of the style of writing found
in college bulletins—a style characterized by brevity and solemnity,
as a rule.

Parody of a Genre

Bob and Ray, the celebrated radio comedians, are to a large degree
parodists, spoofing news commentators, commercials, and soap operas,

among other things. The selection below is from "Garish Summit," their parody of the soap opera genre:

> MAN: *Quite a place you've got here.*
>
> RODNEY: *Thank you. We like it. We have forty-six thousand, two hundred square feet here in the main house. Then, the twins live over in the annex, which has...*
>
> AGATHA: *Oh, shut up, Rodney. Whoever this man is, I'm sure he doesn't want to hear you recite a lot of boring figures.*
>
> RODNEY: *You're quite right, Mother. Perhaps introductions would be more in order. I'm the wealthy but spineless young executive, Rodney Murchfield. And this is my dowager mother, Agatha.*
>
> MAN: *Pleased to meet you, Miss Agatha. I've been looking forward to this moment. You see, I'm your long-lost elder son, Skippy.*
>
> *(Organ: musical sting)*

You can see, from the type of characters involved and the plot line, that this selection spoofs the conventions of the soap opera. Audiences in America who are not familiar with soap operas as a genre (if such people exist here) would still find the script amusing, but wouldn't appreciate it as much, I would suggest, as those who recognize the intertextual aspects of the script.

Parody of a Text

A text, such as a short story, a film, a novel, or a poem has to be famous and familiar to large numbers of people to be susceptible to parody. It also has to have a distinctive identity: characters who have peculiarities, certain kinds of events, and so on. The parody must play with these characters and stay close to them. For example, James Bond novels, in general, and specific works such as *Dr. No*, lend themselves to parody.

The same applies to familiar poems, such as "Trees" and "Twinkle, Twinkle, Little Star." A parody of this "Twinkle, Twinkle" poem follows:

> *Scintillate, scintillate, globule vivific,*
> *Fain would I fathom thy nature specific.*
> *Loftily poised in ether capacious,*
> *Strongly resembling a gem carbonaceous.*

The humor stems from the "citation" aspects of the poem and the use of esoteric (technical, scientific) language.

Parody has a long history; as Bakhtin points out in his book on Rabelais, during the Middle Ages there were numerous parodies of religious writings and other texts. As he writes in *Rabelais and His World* (1984, 84):

> Medieval parody, especially before the twelfth century, was not concerned with the negative, the imperfections of specific cults, ecclesiastic orders, or scholars which could be the object of derision and destruction. For the medieval parodist everything was without exception comic. Laughter was as universal as seriousness; it was directed at the whole world, at history, at all societies, at ideology. It was the world's second truth extended to everything and from which nothing is taken away. It was, as it were, the festive aspect of the whole world in all its elements, the second revelation of the world in play and laughter.

There were parodies, he adds, of church dramas, fairy tales, debates, animal epics, and so forth, and the carnival rituals and spectacles were also parodic in nature. All of this was in opposition to official Christian church culture and doctrine and was, interestingly enough, officially sanctioned.

Of course, there were parodies in ancient times as well. So parody is nothing new and parody is one of the most important techniques utilized by humorists, though we must remember that parody itself uses a variety of other techniques such as ridicule and exaggeration.

Conclusions

A great deal of humor, we must recognize, is not transmitted verbally (as in jokes and witticisms) but physically—by facial expression, body language, crazy noises, and ridiculous props. Clowns are case studies in semiotic excess: they push all signs to their very limits. They violate the codes of normalcy and flexibility just the way comic types such as misers, hypochondriacs, and blusterers do.

In the case of jokes, a semiotic perspective yields two kinds of analysis. A syntagmatic analysis examines the narrative structure of the joke and shows how the punch line leads to a new meaning being placed on the events that preceded the punch line. An opposition of sorts is set up between what we might have anticipated and the incongruous outcome we get. A paradigmatic analysis examines a joke text in terms of the paired oppositions implicit in the text that give it meaning.

Figurative devices such as metaphor and metonymy also play a role in humor, since they are the mechanisms behind two important techniques of humor: analogy and stereotyping. I have suggested that the arbitrary relation between the signifier and signified may be analogous to the arbitrary relation between the narrative events in a joke and its incongruous punch line. Puns, from a semiotic perspective, can be seen as a form of wordplay in which a signifier can be used, on the basis of sound, to stand for either of two signifieds. It is this ambivalence that is the basis of good puns; if there is only a play on sound, the pun is not a good one. Finally, the role of parody was discussed, with reference to its long history and to its various forms: parodies of authorial style, parodies of genres, and parodies of well-known texts.

References

Allen, Woody. "Spring Bulletin." *Getting Even*. New York: Vintage Books, 1978.

Attardo, Salvatore, and Jean-Charles Chabanne. "Jokes as a Text Type." In *Humor*, vol. 5, nos. 1/2, 1992.

Bakhtin, Mikhail. *Rabelais and His World*. Translated by Helen Iswolsky. Bloomington: Indiana University Press, 1984.

Bouissac, Paul. "A Semiotic Approach to Nonsense: Clowns and Limericks." In Thomas A. Sebeok, ed. *Sight, Sound and Sense*. Bloomington: Indiana University Press, 1978.

Elliot, Bob, and Ray Goulding. *From Approximately Coast to Coast It's the Bob and Ray Show*. New York: Penguin Books, 1985.

Norrick, Neal R. "Intertextuality in Humor." In *Humor*, vol. 2, no. 2, 1989.

*Comedy and tragedy both sprang from
parallel, if not identical origins—insofar as
the classicists have been able to explore
them, from sacrificial feasts and other
religious ceremonies. Each rite had its myth
in due season and the play-acting formed
part of the celebration. To his tutelary altar
in the orchestra, that dancing-place of the
original Greek theatre, Dionysius, the
ecstatic god, brought with him the choric
adjuncts of wine, women, and song in early
spring. Comedy has been traced back to the
revel, or komos, which in turn looks ahead to
the Aristophanic finale, the wedding or
gamos. Phallephoric processions, orgiastic
dances featuring satyrs rather than heroes,
were a comic counterpart to the stately
tragic dithyrambs, which had fostered
panegyric rather than invective. Revelry—
licensed disorder, sometimes proclaimed by
obscenities—was the scheduled order of the
day; and the date was perforce a holiday, as
it would be with the Saturnalia in Rome, and
with the analagous seasons of carnival in
other cultures, when the conventional
observances of society were relaxed and even
reversed for a topsy-turvy interim.*

> —Harry Levin
>   *Playboys & Killjoys: An Essay on
>   the Theory and Practice of Comedy*

6

From Carnival to Comedy:
Literary Theory and Humor

Many literary and subliterary works are humorous or have a substantial amount of humor in them. We have, for example, humorous novels, humorous plays (comedies), humorous poetry, humorous comic strips, and humorous greeting cards. I call a text humorous if it is meant to evoke laughter, in contrast to texts meant to evoke tears or some kind of a recognition of our allegedly "tragic" fate or destiny. In this chapter I will be dealing with everything from medieval carnivals to the nature of comedy and what it is that makes characters "humorous." I will also use the term in a more conventional sense—to mean anything funny and meant to amuse and cause laughter.

Medieval Perspectives on Humor

In medieval times it was held that there were four fluids in the body—blood, phlegm, choler, and black bile—and that one of these fluids always dominated in a given individual, shaping his or her physical body, basic personality, and temperament. Mikhail Bakhtin, in his classic study *Rabelais and His World,* suggests that humor was connected to the medieval carnival, a festive sense of life and the mind-set of the common folk. As he writes (1984, 4):

> A boundless world of humorous forms and manifestations opposed the official and serious tone of medieval ecclesiastical and feudal culture. In spite of their variety, folk festivities of the carnival type, the clowns and fools, giants, dwarfs, and jugglers, the vast and manifold literature of parody—all these forms have one style in common: they belong to one culture of folk carnival humor.

This sensibility manifested itself in such forms as comic pageants, comic verbal texts (in Latin and the vernacular), and numerous kinds of billingsgate. In this period, he adds, we find such things as the "feast of fools," parish feasts and fairs, and a general atmosphere of gaiety and laughter.

Carnival, for Bakhtin is not something that people observe from a distance, so to speak, but is something that pervades their everyday lives. Everyone participates in it and it embraces everyone. When carnival exists, he continues, there is no law outside it; it is subject only to its own laws. This folk humor, he adds, is not similar to the negative and formal parody found in modern texts; folk humor for Bakhtin is not negative; it makes fun of institutions, but at the same time it revives and renews them. It also influenced the medieval comic theater.

Bakhtin's theory of carnivalization has been very influential and contemporary critics have used it in a number of ways. Some have focused on carnivalization as a means of contrasting the joy and sense of excitement that existed in medieval life with the sterility and alienation found in many contemporary societies. Others use it as a way of legitimating studies of popular culture. The title of Bakhtin's book on Rabelais actually uses the term *popular culture* in the Russian edition and this gives his work a slightly different cast and shows he gives more importance to popular culture than the English translation of his book title does.

Laughter in the Renaissance and Seventeenth Century

In the Renaissance, Bakhtin suggests, there was a positive sense of what laughter was and what its function was. He writes (1984, 66):

> Laughter has a deep philosophical meaning, it is one of the essential forms of truth concerning the world as a whole, concerning history and man; it is a peculiar point of view relative to the world; the world is seen anew, no less (and perhaps more) profoundly than when seen from the serious standpoint. Therefore, laughter is just as admissible in great literature, posing universal problems, as seriousness. Certain essential aspects of the world are accessible only to laughter.

By the seventeenth century, however, people's view of laughter had changed, Bakhtin suggests. Humor was not seen as universal and a source of wisdom and truth. Instead it was seen as an individual matter and one that dealt only with typical aspects of social life—that is, it essentially focused on private and social vices. Humor, it was thought, could not deal with important themes and belonged only to low genres. It could, therefore, only be a light amusement dealing with the lives of people who belonged to inferior social levels.

To a certain degree, a post Renaissance view of laughter has been the one that has dominated our thinking about humor and humorous literary works. We have tended to assume that if something is funny, it can't be important or significant. Ironically, for Bakhtin, laughter is not so much the opposite of seriousness but a phenomenon that purifies and completes seriousness, that liberates it from fanaticism, prevents seriousness from atrophying, from didacticism, and from sentimentality. Bakhtin's notion of carnival and his books on Rabelais and literary theory have been extremely important and have led, one might say, to renewed interest in the study of humor and humorous texts in all media and all genres, high as well as low. That is, it is now seen as perfectly acceptable to study popular culture as well as elite culture—though many critics (postmodernist and otherwise) now suggest the differences between these two kinds of culture are minimal, if there are any differences at all.

On Comedy and Tragedy

Ferdinand de Saussure, in his *Course in General Linguistics,* pointed out that concepts gain their meaning differentially. "Concepts," he writes, "are purely differential and defined not by their positive content but negatively by their relations with the other terms of the system" (1966, 117). It is not content, per se, that determines what something means but, rather, its relations in the system in which it is embedded. As he writes, the "most precise characteristic" of these concepts "is in being what the others are not" (1966, 117).

Thus, to understand what comedy is, we must know what comedy isn't, and we can best find out, I would suggest, by comparing it with the dramatic form that is most different from it, namely, tragedy. If comedy deals with low types, common folk, as post Renaissance theorists argued it must, then tragedy must deal with high types, superior figures such as kings and great men and women. These lower elements generally survive while the higher elements are destroyed, often carried off the stage dead, as everyone on stage laments. That is, comedy has a happy ending (in which confusions of all sorts are resolved) and tragedy has a sad ending (in which the resolutions are not happy by any means).

Comedy traditionally has been held to deal with the social and tragedy with the personal or individual—the fall of a great figure as the result of chance but also often as the result of hubris. Some argue that tragedy can also involve the fall of an archetypical common man or woman, such as Willy Loman. Comedy generates laughter and feelings of optimism and ebullience, while tragedy generates pity and tears. Comedies often involve lovers who are frustrated for one reason or another, but finally get together; the comedy ends with various loose ends being tied up and with a festive celebration, frequently a marriage. In tragedy, on the other hand, lovers end up separated, at the least, and frequently one or both die, sometimes by their own hands. There's a kind of relentless logic to tragedy, as events move to their inevitable end. In comedy, on the other hand, there is chance and confusion. Comedies facilitate the release of libidinal energy, cathexis, while tragedies produce a profound experience of empathy and a sense of understanding of the human situation, namely, a catharsis.

We can see the differences by listing the basic attributes of comedy and tragedy, with the caveat that we are making very broad generalizations and many texts do not fit under one or the other in a precise way.

COMEDY	TRAGEDY
Optimism	Pessimism
Social phenomena	Personal
Comic types	Individuals
Laughter	Tears
Low status individuals	High status individuals
Chance	Inevitability
Survival	Death
Wedding	Funeral
Cathexis	Catharsis

While this chart has its limitations, it does offer us a general perspective, one might say, on the difference between comedy and tragedy.

In an essay "Comedy, Humor, the Ode" we find another difference between comedy and tragedy. Comedies are much more complex than tragedies, whose plots move inexorably and in a rather direct way toward their conclusion. As Burke writes (1964, 86):

> Comedy requires the maximum of forensic complexity. In the tragic plot the *deus ex machina* is always lurking, to give events a fatalistic turn in accordance with the old *"participation"* pattern whereby men anthropomorphize nature, feeling its force as the taking sides with them or against them. Comedy must develop logical forensic causality to its highest point, calling not upon astronomical marvels to help shape the plot, but completing the process of internal organization whereby each event is deduced "syllogistically" from the premises of the informing situation.

Comedy deals with *man in society,* tragedy with *cosmic man.* ... Comedy is essentially *humane,* leading in periods of comparative stability to the comedy of manners, the dramatization of quirks and foibles. But it is not necessarily confined to drama. The best of Bentham, Marx, and Veblen is high comedy.

This helps explain why comedies are often so complicated. Some kind of a confusing mess is created in comedies and the characters have to figure out ways of extricating themselves from the mess, tying up all the loose ends, and resolving things in a satisfactory way. What makes things difficult is that our comic characters are, so often, bizarre. Some are monomaniacs, some are fools, and the realistic characters, usually young lovers, have to figure out how to deal with them.

Burke's comment about Bentham, Marx, and Veblen reminds us that comedy is not confined to dramatic forms but that writers who are satirical and sarcastic, who ridicule and insult, among other things, also can be seen as humorists.

Comedy and the Reversed Oedipus Complex

There are many different kinds of comedy as an examination of the history of comedy over the centuries shows; it has countless forms and manifestations. Still, dramatic comedies frequently deal with a beautiful young woman and a handsome young man who are in love and despite difficulties (often posed by an old man, who has his own plans for the woman) manage to outwit the *senex* and his associates and get married.

In an essay entitled "The Argument of Comedy," Northrop Frye points out that there is an Oedipal dimension to much comedy. He discusses Greek comedy and makes a distinction between Old Comedy, the eleven plays written by Aristophanes, and New Comedy, written by Menander, Plautus, and Terrence. New Comedy often has what Frye describes as a comic Oedipus situation in which a young man gets to possess the young woman of his choice by outwitting an older opponent, usually the father or guardian of the girl but also often a wealthy older man, who desires the young woman for himself.

Martin Grotjahn describes this phenomenon as the "reversed" Oedipus Complex and mentions, in this respect, an essay by Ludwig Jekels, "The Origin of Comedy." According to Jekels, in comedy we find an inversion of the Oedipus Complex: it is the father, not the son, who is guilty. As Grotjahn writes:

> The villain is the victim of his own villainy; the cheat is cheated....The son is not impotent, but the father is impotent, castrated, conquered. The son does not compete; but the weak and ridiculous father tries to do all the things which the son tried to do in the original tragic setting of the drama. The son plays the role of the father and the father is cast in the role of the son. The result is amused superiority, laughing aggression, triumph without remorse, guilt, or fear of punishment. (1966, 86)

We find a number of reversals of the Oedipus theme.

In the original story, Oedipus (without recognizing what he has done) kills his father and marries a woman, Jocasta, who turns out to be his mother. In the inversion, a father or father figure tries to interfere with the sex life of his son, or some young man, and, perhaps, gain some desirable young woman for himself. This situation, Grotjahn suggests, happens to all men as they get older and see young men taking over. In real life, Grotjahn adds, the relationship between a father and son can generally be worked out harmoniously and the outcome of the Oedipal struggle between generations can result in a drawing together of son and father. But in comedy, this is not the case and one of the reasons we enjoy comedy is that it enables us to see the variety of ways in which older men, father figures, *senex* figures, can be defeated by their younger rivals. Just as the son tried to witness lovemaking between his parents, now the father (and older men who are father figures) tries to prevent lovemaking between his son and some woman.

Frye wrote his essay in the late 1940s. He suggested that most movie comedies were, basically, New Comedies, with minor modifications here and there. And though there have been many changes in films since Frye wrote his essay, it probably still is a valid generalization. Comedy, we must remember, evolved from the *komos,* a revel, a processional dance, that looked forward to the *gamos* or wedding. So the roots of comedy are in festivity, love, and sex and modern theatrical comedies, film comedies, and television comedies often concern themselves with these topics. Or, in the case of situation comedies on television, they concern themselves with life after the happy marriage.

On Humors and Comic Types

The theory of humors, mentioned earlier, suggests that each individual is dominated by one of the four fluids or humors found in people. This leads, logically, to the notion that comedies deal with types of people or with people who are ruled by some specific passion. Ben Jonson described this phenomenon in his "Induction" to *Everyman and His Humour,* which was written in 1599 (Levin, 1987, 183), as follows:

> Some one peculiar quality
> Doth so possess a man, that it doth draw
> All his affects, his spirits, and his powers
> In their confluctions, all to run one way.

This notion of personality types has played an important role in comedy.

In "The Argument of Comedy," Frye points out that the hero of a comedy frequently finds himself battling one or more comic types. He writes (Felheim, 1962, 237–38):

> These are always people who are in some kind of mental bondage, who are help-lessly driven by ruling passions, neurotic compulsions, social rituals, and selfish-ness. The miser, the hypochondriac, the hypocrite, the pedants, the snob: these are humors, people who do not fully know what they are doing, who are slaves to a predictable self-imposed pattern of behavior. What we call the moral norm is, then, not morality but deliverance from moral bondage. Comedy is designed not to con-demn evil, but to ridicule lack of self-knowledge.

What this means, Frye continues, is that comic resolutions involve both an individual release and a social reconciliation. We find two releases: a normal individual escapes the bond of a humorous society (that is, one made up of people who are zany monomaniacs) and a normal society is freed from bonds imposed on it by these humorous individuals.

There are a number of basic comic types according to Frye. Some of the most important of these are: *alazons* or blusterers and imposters; *eirons* or dissemblers and self-deprecators; *bomolochoi* or buffoons; and *agroikos* or churlish rustics. There is a logical opposition between the *alazons,* who pretend they are more than they really are, and the *eirons,* who pretend they are less than they are.

In *Playboys and Killjoys: An Essay on the Theory and Practice of Comedy,* Harry Levin points out that comic types are still in use. He mentions that Chinese Opera, probably the most conventionalized the-ater, uses four basic characters: a *sheng* or male lead; a *dan* or female lead, conventionally played by a man; a *jing* or heavy; and a *chou* or clown. He adds that English and American stock companies have a stan-dard cast of characters. These are, he writes (1987, 65–66): "The Lead-ing Man and Lady, the Juvenile, the Ingenue, the Heavy, the Low Comedian, the Soubrette, the First and Second Walking Gentlemen."

Such types help us because they provide us, instantaneously, with a sense of who a given character is and what his or her motivations might be.

There is, then, a formulaic quality to comedy, as a rather standard cast of character types interact with one another. We know what the characters are like but we don't know what kind of a mess they will create or how they will extricate themselves from this mess. Levin quotes a humorous poem from the age of Queen Anne about the types of characters one finds in comedies, which shows how formulaic they were, and how much they relied on character types (1987, 66):

> The Fop, the Rake, the Country Squire and Cit,
> The Real Blockhead and Conceited Wit,
> The Jilting Mistress and the Faithless Wife,
> Shall see themselves all painted to the life.
> —William Taverner

The significance of comic types dates back as far as Old Comedy in Greece. In his book, *The People of Aristophanes: A Sociology of Old Attic Comedy,* Victor Ehrenberg points out that in Old Comedy, people in the plays are not individuals but "types." He writes (1962, 40):

> The type, once fixed, needed little change or improvement. There was no need to create it anew; it existed and had early become a permanent factor in comedy. ...The complete range of types was not crystallized till the time of Menander. But already in the first comedy of Aristophanes, the *Daitales,* two pairs of types appear: the good and the bad son, and (as later in the *Clouds*) the conservative father and his modern-minded son. This shows that not only single persons but also pairs or, less commonly, social groups could become typical, and so lead to the creation of stock motifs and scenes.

This is an interesting insight because it explains the way we are able to make ethnic groups or members of professions into "types" and ridicule them, in ethnic jokes about Jews and Poles and in jokes about doctors and lawyers, for example. We find, then, that in ancient Greece, stereotyping groups of people for comic purposes existed, and it remains with us today. Interestingly enough, we also find that the battle between the conservative father and the modern-minded son is an old one.

It is easy to understand the creation of pairs of types when you think back to Saussure's discussion of concepts and how they only maintain their meaning differentially; if you provide characters who represent two opposing character or personality types, you help define and establish the typicality of each member of the pair. It is relevant here to mention, once again, Henri Bergson's theories about comic types, found in his essay *Laughter*. Bergson was discussed in the chapter on philosophy and humor but his insights are of some utility here, also. He suggests that human beings become laughable to the extent that their movements and gestures remind us of machines, since humor occurs when the mechanical is "encrusted" or superimposed upon the living. If our bodies, somehow, are made to resemble machines, we find the situation humorous.

This notion has obvious implications for the matter of humor and personality types. People who are rigid, who are inflexible, remind us, so his theory suggests, of machines. Bergson writes:

> Every comic character is a *type*. Inversely, every resemblance to a type has something comic in it....It is comic to fall into a ready-made category. And what is most comic of all is to become a category oneself into which others will fall, as into a ready-made frame; it is to crystallize into a stock character. (1956, 156–57)

Comedy, he adds, not only gives us stock types but comedy is the only kind of art "that aims at the general." He sees rigidity, which forces characters to keep strictly to a given path, to pursue their passions with a singlemindedness, as at the heart of comedy.

This rigidity in the personality of comic characters, their monomania, might suggest that there is an element of the inexorable in comedy as well as in tragedy. It has been suggested that there is no freedom for characters in tragedies who must inevitably go to their death and destruction. The difference here is that the monomaniacs are figures of ridicule who play out their roles in an ambience of festivity and joyfulness. Also, they are generally not the central characters of comedies, though they may have large roles in them; it is the lovers, the young man and the young woman, who are the center of attention. The comic characters tend to have secondary roles, though of course in some comedies the lovers are themselves comic types. (Kate, for example, is a shrew in *The Taming of the Shrew*.)

In tragedies, on the other hand, it is the doomed heroes and heroines who are the focus of attention and with whom members of an audience empathize. In comedy we find all these rigid types defeated, so that comedy is an argument for flexibility and openness to possibilities. This may explain why we find comedy so delicious. It provides the sense of liberation and freedom so often mentioned by authors who espouse psychoanalytic theories of humor.

Conclusions

Comedies have been with us for a long time (Aristophanes wrote his famous comedy *The Birds* in 414 B.C., for example) and because comedy and humor play such a large role in literature—conceived broadly to cover texts such as plays, poems, novels, and popular genres—literary scholars have written a considerable amount about humor (though not as much as the subject deserves). But until recently those who wrote about comedy more often than not did so because of personal passions and in spite of the mindset found in academia that humor was a relatively trivial matter—as was popular culture. Humor was not taken seriously (it sounds strange to say this) and popular culture was ignored because so many people loved it!

This notion that humor was relatively unimportant existed in many English and literature departments in spite of the fact that many of the world's greatest dramas, novels, and so on are humorous works. Thanks to Bakhtin and others, things have changed considerably, and humor and popular culture are being given the attention they deserve. The zanies, monomaniacs, and eccentric types we found in the Greek comedies and other comedies that came after them still are, it is comforting to know, found in contemporary dramas as well—and in our films, situation comedies, comic strips, and other mass-mediated texts. And *senexes* still roam the halls of academe, interfering in the lives of assistant professors, but that is another matter—for the alienist rather than the literary scholar.

References

Bakhtin, Mikhail. *Rabelais and His World*. Translated by Helene Iswolsky. Bloomington: Indiana University Press, 1984.

Burke, Kenneth. *Terms for Order*. Edited by Stanley Edgar Hyman. Bloomington: Indiana University Press, 1964.

Ehrenberg, Victor. *The People of Aristophanes*. New York: Schocken Books, 1962.

Felheim, Marvin, ed. *Comedy: Plays, Theory, and Criticism*. New York: Harcourt Brace & World, 1962.

Grotjahn, Martin. *Beyond Laughter: Humor and the Subconscious*. New York: McGraw-Hill, 1966.

Levin, Harry. *Playboys and Killjoys: An Essay on the Theory & Practice of Comedy*. New York: Oxford University Press, 1987.

Saussure, Ferdinand de. *Course in General Linguistics*. New York: McGraw Hill, 1966.

Sypher, Wylie, ed. *Comedy*. New York: Anchor Books, 1956.

Humor *is therefore defined as a social message intended to produce laughter or smiling. As with any social message, it fulfills certain functions, uses special techniques, has a content, and is used in certain situations. These aspects of humor can be understood as relating to the questions of* why *people use humor (its functions),* how it *is transmitted (techniques),* what *it communicates (content), and* where and when *it is communicated (situation). Some of these aspects of humor are universal, characterizing humor everywhere. Others are more influenced by culture.*

—Avner Ziv
National Styles of Humor

7

The Functions of Laughter:
Sociological Aspects of Humor

When we look at humor from a sociological point of view we run into a big problem, for, it can be argued, there is no such thing as sociology, per se. It has, Irving Louis Horowitz suggests, "decomposed" or fragmented itself so much that all one can say (without stretching things too far) is that there are people, with widely varying approaches to the study of society, who call themselves sociologists. As he writes in *The Decomposition of Sociology* (1993, 12):

> [S]ociology has largely become a repository of discontent, a gathering of individuals who have special agendas, from gay and lesbian rights to liberation theology. But this has accelerated the decomposition process. Any notion of a common democratic culture or a universal scientific base has become suspect. Ideologists masked as sociologists attack it as a dangerous form of bourgeois objectivism or, worse, as an imperialist pretension. In this climate, sociology has lost meaning apart from its ideological roots and pseudoscientific posturing.

He notes that social scientists who once identified themselves as sociologists have, as it were, been abandoning the sinking ship—urbanologists, demographers, criminologists, and so on.

Given this situation, I have taken one of the core notions of sociological thought—functionalism—to use for my case study of how a relatively traditional sociological thinker might deal with humor. One of the main questions this kind of sociologist would ask is: What are the functions of humor for various groups in society? Who uses humor, for what purposes, and to what effects?

Defining Functionalism

Functionalism, as I will use the term, is a perspective that considers what role an entity plays in helping maintain some group. Here I am following Thompson, Ellis, and Wildavsky, who suggest that earlier functional explanations, which were offered for society in general, were too broad. As they write in *Cultural Theory* (1990, 106):

> Perhaps the most debilitating error made by past practitioners of functional explanation was to look for functions that went with entire societies. The assumption that behavior that is functional for some individuals and groups within a society is necessarily functional for all left functional analysis wide open to criticism that it neglected conflict.

This societal perspective didn't ask who benefits from a given pattern of so-called functional behavior because it tried to suggest that all of society did, but the more limited perspective offered above recognizes that what is functional for one way of life often is dysfunctional and undermines other ways of life.

Functionalism is also, our authors suggest, ideologically neutral, though functionalists in the past often had ideologically conservative perspectives on things. In addition, by tying it to ways of life, functionalism can also deal with conflict. Functions can be positive and help maintain the group, or they can be negative and serve to break up the group. In some cases, an action has no effect, in which case it is described as nonfunctional.

Functional analysts also make a number of distinctions relative to our awareness of functions. Manifest functions are those functions that are intended and we are aware of. But latent functions are functions that we are not aware of and have unintended consequences. (Some have suggested that political science is the study of manifest functions and sociology is the study of latent, unintended consequences, which are, in many respects it can be argued, the most interesting kind.)

Finally, there is the concept of functional alternatives, which states that certain functions can be taken care of in a number of different ways by different activities or institutions. For example, humor may be thought of as a functional alternative (in certain situations) to physical violence. Instead of hitting someone, we use humor to assuage our aggressive impulses and hostile feelings.

Let me list these different aspects of functionalism below:

Functional:	Helps maintain some way of life
Dysfunctional:	Helps break down some way of life
Nonfunctional:	Has no impact on a way of life
Manifest Functions:	Done consciously for a given purpose

Latent Functions: Unintended consequences of which we
                          are unaware
Functional Alternative: Other ways of doing something

With these distinctions in mind we can better understand how functionalists deal with humor. Thus, two sociologists, Chris Powell and George E. C. Paton, edited a book, *Humour in Society,* whose central theme is "the use of humour by social actors as a means of social control or resistance to such control." That is, the various articles deal with the functions of humor for different groups, occupations, subcultures, and so on. Humor can be used, the authors add, as an important "social indicator of historical developments and social changes" (1988, xix).

Powell and Paton make an important point: that humor is not to be equated with jokes. (I make this point a number of times in this book.) The articles in their book contain a large number of jokes, but this is because, they write, jokes are short and relatively easy to deal with. But we should not equate humor with jokes and joke telling. They quote a line from Trevor Griffith's play, *The Comedians,* to the effect that "It's not the jokes. It's what lies behind 'em. It's the attitude" (Faber, 1976, 20). It is, then, the attitudes, beliefs, and values that are reflected in humor that are of concern to Powell and Paton—especially since jokes and humor involve either social control or resistance to control. This humor, they add, is often found in graffiti, wordplay, cartoons, gestures, facial expressions, comic postures and walks, sounds, and so on. Humor is not confined to any one form of expression or genre.

A Case Study: Stupid Outsiders

In his article "Stupidity and Rationality: Jokes from the Iron Cage," Christie Davies deals with jokes about so-called stupid groups in societies—Poles (in America), Irish (in England), and so on. Let me offer several examples of jokes here, taken from his article, which appeared in *Humour in Society.* This is a joke told in the United States:

A Polish couple decided to have a chicken farm. They bought two chickens, took them home, dug a hole in their backyard and buried the chickens head first. Next morning they discovered the chickens were dead.

They bought two more chickens, this time planting them in the ground feet down. By the next morning the fowl had died. They wrote to the Polish consulate explaining their problem. Within a week they received a prompt reply from the Polish consul. The letter said "Please send us a soil sample."

This is a joke told in Great Britain:

Article in Irish medical journal: "Are vasectomies hereditary?"

Just about every Western industrialized country, he points out, and many other countries as well, has some "stupid" group that it makes jokes about.

These jokes have a number of functions, Davies suggests. They enable members of the society, at large, to distance themselves from the marginalized stupid group, and enable people to reassure themselves that as ordinary members of society, they are intelligent and rational. There have always been jokes about stupid people and groups, such as the foolish inhabitants of Chelm, for instance. But as Davies points out, these groups existed in agricultural communities whereas the Polish and Irish jokes and other jokes about stupid minorities flourish in industrialized societies.

This is probably because, he writes, we have a need in modern, technological societies to feel positive about our contemporary institutions. As he puts it:

> At one level, then, we may see jokes about stupid outsiders as an affirmation of the value of rationality, efficiency, and applied intelligence on the part of the joke-tellers, for any failure to live up to and conform to these qualities is ascribed to outsiders and then subjected to severe ridicule....By apportioning implicit praise and direct mockery in this way, the jokes act as a minor means of social control. They are one more factor pressing individuals into conformity with the "rational" demands of modern organizations and society. (Davies, 1988, 4)

In addition, these jokes help people deal with various forms of anxiety they face in modern, rational, industrialized societies by creating a peripheral ethnic minority of stupid people to whom one can feel superior.

At the same time they provide a moment of release from the imperatives of this society, from the "iron cage" Max Weber talked about in describing the impact of Puritanism on American society, in which we would be "specialists without spirit, sensualists without heart" (Davies, 1988, 11). Ethnic jokes about stupid nationalities (Poles in America, the Irish in Great Britain, Belgians in France, Norwegians and Finns in Sweden, etc.) are popular because they have a number of functions for those who tell such jokes—not merely because they are humorous. (Many people of course, especially members of the ethnic groups being ridiculed, would not find them funny at all.)

The manifest function of telling jokes about dumb Poles and stupid Irishmen would be to amuse people, to be funny. But there are many other kinds of jokes one can tell to amuse others. Thus, it would seem that the latent functions of these jokes—to gain a sense of superiority, to assuage feelings of anxiety in complex, industrialized societies, and to exert subtle social control—are what is really of significance here. All of this is done without the persons telling these jokes about stupid sub-groups being aware of what they are really doing.

If these jokes are functional for some groups, they are, according to our understanding of functionalism, dysfunctional for members of the groups being identified as stupid, leading to negative self-images, per-haps even self-hatred, and other things. That is why ethnic humor has been, more or less, banished from the media, though ethnic humor ex-ists and flourishes in folklore, where people generally feel free to ex-press themselves without regard for social opinion or even internal self-censorship.

Humor and Social Integration

Humor also functions as a means of social integration. It helps people integrate themselves in groups and helps groups establish identity and a sense of solidarity. Hugh C. Foot and Antony Chapman discuss what they call "social laughter" in "The Social Responsiveness of Young Children in Humorous Situations" and write that it:

> is a means of gaining social approval, bolstering group cohesiveness and signal-ling our affiliative motives. It is also used in maintaining the flow of interaction in our daily encounters: filling in pauses in our conversations and maintaining the interest and attention of our conversational partner. (1976, 188)

Humor, then, plays an important role in our everyday lives and is not confined to joke telling or specific situations where a person tries to amuse an individual or a group of people.

They add that in some situations we use humor to ridicule others (what they call "derision laughter") and point out that this is often found in chil-dren who use it to mock others or to direct attention away from their own shortcomings. Adults also use this kind of humor, typically in the form of sarcastic comments or allusions to embarrassing situations that others have been involved in. If people show offense at this derisive humor, the hu-morist can always counter that the remarks were made in jest.

This leads to an important aspect of humor: It enables people to say things that ordinarily they would not be able, for a variety of reasons, to say. In earlier periods there were fools and court jesters who were given this privilege, and for good reason. In "The Disinhibiting Effects of Humor: Aggressive and Affective Response" Avner Ziv and Orit Gadish explain the role of jesters and the matter of saying "I was only joking" as enabling people to transgress taboos and social barriers. As they write:

> The best historical example can be found in the old institution of the court jester. During the Middle Ages, most monarchs and other powerful figures in Europe had a court jester who was allowed to say even the most forbidden things in public, even to criticize his employer. The jester enjoyed a privileged status. (1990, 247)

So jester figures had important functions in the Middle Ages in the same way that the functional alternatives or analogues of these jesters, our humorists and comedians, also have important functions. They find themselves allowed—perhaps required—to say forbidden things about the rich and powerful and they are very well rewarded for their efforts. Ordinary people assume the role of jesters at times and defend themselves from criticism by saying "I was only kidding."

Jesters and comedians function as safety valves, allowing people to express resentments and thus vent their anger and hostility verbally instead of taking action. Swearing has a similar function: it enables people to deal with their anger verbally instead of through physical violence.

On Uses and Gratifications

This discussion of the various functions of humor leads to an approach that is, it could be said, an applied form of functionalism, namely, uses and gratifications theory. Unlike many communication theorists who study the effects that mass-mediated texts (such as television shows, comic books, jokes, etc.) have on audiences, the uses and gratification theorists study the way people use texts and the gratifications these texts offer people.

We decide to watch certain television shows—a certain situation comedy, a variety show, a talk show—because we get a number of gratifications from each show and we use the show for specific purposes, though we probably are seldom aware of what we are doing. Most people would say they like a show because they find it entertaining or amusing or something vague like that. The question then arises: Why this show and not that show? Saying that a television show is entertaining or amusing is too vague, too broad, too much of a generalization. What uses and gratifications theory does is allow us to pinpoint which specific uses and gratifications a text offers (or may be offering) to individuals or groups.

Elihu Katz and some colleagues mention some of the work that has been done on this matter relative to the mass media. They discuss the work of

> Herzog (1942) on quiz programs and the gratifications derived from listening to soap operas; Suchman (1942) on the motives for getting interested in serious music on radio; Wolfe and Fiske (1949) on the development of children's interests in comics; Berelson (1949) on the functions of newspaper reading; and so on. Each of these investigations came up with a list of functions served either by some specific contents or by the medium in question: to match one's wits against others, to get information or advice for daily living, to provide a framework for one's day, to prepare oneself culturally for the demands of upward mobility, or to be reassured about the dignity and usefulness of one's role. (Katz et al. 1979)

Thus, a text can serve a number of different uses (that is, functions) for individuals and groups and provide a number of different gratifications (that is, rewards).

Let me offer a list of some of the more important uses and gratifications that sociologists and other scholars have mentioned in various articles. Presumably, a given individual (or, members of some group with values and attitudes in common) would find some of these uses and gratifications important and, without necessarily being aware of their role, would by guided by them in choosing television shows to watch, films to see, humor to enjoy, or jokes to tell. The uses and gratifications listed below have been revised and tailored to apply to humor, jokes, and related concerns:

1. To be made to laugh.
2. To feel superior to others, who are seen as stupid or foolish.
3. To see authority figures deflated.
4. To have shared experiences (of laughter) with others.
5. To experience guilt-free aggression and hostility.
6. To see others make mistakes.
7. To be purged of unpleasant feelings through laughter.
8. To obtain an outlet for sexual or aggressive drives in a guilt-free manner.
9. To gain an identity.
10. To learn about the world.

11. To find distraction and diversion.
12. To integrate oneself into some group.
13. To cope with embarrassing situations, hostility, etc.
14. To explore taboo subjects without risk.
15. To affirm one's moral, political, and spiritual values.
16. To see comic "villains" in action.
17. To facilitate interpersonal relationships.
18. To cope with stress and anxiety.
19. To show the triumph of justice.
20. To have the pleasure of a momentary regression.
21. To express ideas that otherwise would not be tolerated.

Uses and Gratifications Derived from Humor

You can see from this list (and other uses can be added) that humor can serve a number of different purposes for individuals or groups. When applying these uses and gratifications, it is important to tie each of them, specifically, to events in texts being considered—actions or statements by characters in comedies or jokes. We must show that a given action or statement has a given use or provides a given gratification. One of the problems with this theory is that unless we are actually interviewing people and asking them about texts, much of what we do is hypothetical. That is, we discuss some aspect of a text and show that logically it has (or should have) certain uses or provides certain gratifications.

A Joke and Its Gratifications: A Case Study

Let's put the theory to the test by offering a joke and analyzing the uses and gratifications it might offer a typical person. In reality, of course, different individuals would derive varying gratifications from a given text, depending on their psychological dispositions, group affiliations, and so on. Still, there is reason to argue (especially in the case of mass-mediated texts) that large numbers of people are most likely deriving certain gratifications from what characters do and say in popular shows:

A minister returns to his apartment early one day and finds his wife in bed, nude, and the room filled with cigar smoke. He looks down from his fifth floor window and sees a priest leaving the building, smoking a big cigar. In a fit of rage the minister picks up the refrigerator and throws it down on the priest, killing him.

"What have you done?" someone yells from the street. "You've just killed my priest."
In a fit of despondency, the minister throws himself out the window. Seconds later,

a priest, a minister, and a rabbi appear before an angel. "How did you die?" the angel asks each of them. "It was strange. All of a sudden a refrigerator fell on me and killed me," said the priest. "I threw the refrigerator," says the minister, "and then I jumped to my death because I was so full of remorse." "And how did you die, rabbi?" asks the angel. "You've got me. I was minding my own business, sitting in a refrigerator...."

What are some of the gratifications this joke might offer people? First, it deals with sexual impropriety and shows that adulterers are punished, thus supporting conventional moral values. Second, we see authority figures (priests, ministers, rabbis) deflated and made fun of. The minister's wife is cheating on him and the rabbi is an adulterer who ends up hiding in a refrigerator. Third, it provides a laugh or a moment of amusement and pleasure. Fourth, we see others make mistakes: the minister, killing the innocent priest, and the rabbi, getting caught in an embarrassing situation. Fifth, we see comic "villains" in action—in particular, the rabbi and the minister's wife. Sixth, by dealing with priests, ministers, and rabbis, the joke supports the basic notion that America is a Judeo-Christian country, and thus the joke helps solidify our social or national identities. The joke can also be told with the rabbi's wife and the minister as the adulterers, or the priest and either the rabbi's or minister's wife as adulterers. With the priest as an adulterer, however, it becomes a bit stronger and perhaps would function as a form of revelation about the Catholic church and a means of exploring taboo subjects.

Stereotypes in Humorous Stories about National Character

Finally, let me turn to the way nationalities are represented in humorous stories. I am referring here not to riddles about stupid groups (such as the dumb Poles, Irish, Belgians, Finns, etc.) but humorous stories—technically not jokes, since they don't have punch lines—about the differences between Americans, the French, the Germans, the Russians, the English, and so on. Typically these stories involve the way different nationalities do things: write books about elephants, make love, relate to women when stranded on islands, and that kind of thing. Let me offer a few examples here:

A ship sinks and the survivors find themselves stranded on a desert island. The Americans go into business. The French start night clubs. The Germans build armament plants. After a year the Americans ask the French, "who are those people standing around there?" "They're the English...still waiting to be introduced."

Two men and a young woman are shipwrecked on a desert island. If the men are French, one man will become the woman's husband and the other her lover. If they are Spanish, the men will fight a duel and whoever survives gets the girl. If they are English, nothing will happen because there is nobody to introduce them to one another. If they are Italian, one will murder the other to have the woman for himself. If they are Greek, they will get into an argument about politics and forget about the girl.

UNESCO invites representatives of different countries to a conference on elephants. The following papers are given. The Englishman gives his paper on "Elephant Hunting in Colonial India." The Russian reads "The Superiority of the Russian Elephant." The Italian reads "Elephants and the Renaissance." The Frenchman offers "The Love Life of the Elephant." The German reads "A Short Introduction, in Ten Volumes, to the Study of the Elephant." The American reads "How to Raise Bigger and Better Elephants." An Israeli offers "Elephants and the Jewish Question." A Nigerian offers "Elephants and Racism." The Czechs offer "Why the Soviet Elephant is Our Idol."

These stories, and others like them (such as those about what women say after sexual relations) all deal with popular stereotypes about a number of different nationalities. Similar stories and jokes exist within countries (as in America, where we have jokes about Poles, Jewish American Princesses, etc.) and even within regions, where people from one city make fun of inhabitants of some other city. Thus, Bostonians make fun of New Yorkers, who reciprocate with jokes about Bostonians. In San Francisco Herb Caen, a local gossip columnist, has poked fun at Chico, a small city about 150 miles away, for years.

These stereotypes, like many stereotypes, have an element of truth about them, but they tend to present negative and one-dimensional pictures of the different nationalities being ridiculed. The fact that all the nationalities are made fun of dilutes, I would say, the damage they do, but these stories do perpetuate negative stereotypes and, as such, still may have harmful consequences. Stereotypes are used in popular culture and the mass media because they provide an instant explanation of motivation. If a person is an X, he or she can be expected to act in a certain manner.

From a linguistic standpoint a stereotype is an example of synecdoche. Thus, the American or Frenchman or Italian in the stories stands for all Americans or Frenchman or Italians. And though the stories are humorous, and thus meant to be discounted, they do characterize a large number of people in an obviously simplistic and reductionistic manner. Our amusement at these stories is tied to their use of stereotypes (a basic technique of generating humor) but also to what they say about the "human situation," namely, that we are *all* flawed and comical, in one way or another. Thus, they help us recognize our limitations (and our role in the "human comedy") and make it possible to face life's absurdities with a degree of equanimity.

Conclusions

Our examination of humor from a functionalist perspective has shown that humor can be used to do a variety of things: it can be used to control people, it can be used to resist control and domination, it can help people integrate themselves into groups, it offers "stupid outsiders" to laugh at (and feel superior to), and it offers numerous gratifications to people. It frequently makes use of stereotypes of groups, which provides, on one hand, a quick sense of character and motivation, and on the other negative self-images that are dysfunctional for the group being ridiculed. When analyzing humor we must remember to consider not only the manifest but also the latent functions of the humor.

References

Chapman, Tony, and Hugh Foot, eds. *Humour and Laughter: Theory, Research and Applications*. London: John Wiley & Sons, 1976.

Horowitz, Irving Louis. *The Decomposition of Sociology*. New York: Oxford University Press, 1993.

Katz, Elihu, et al. "Utilization of Mass Communication by the Individual." In Gary Gumpert and Robert Cathcart. *Inter-Media*. New York: Oxford University Press, 1979.

Powell, Chris, and George E. C. Paton, eds. *Humour in Society: Resistance and Control*. New York: St. Martin's Press, 1988.

Thompson, Michael, Richard Ellis, and Aaron Wildavsky. *Cultural Theory*. Boulder, CO: Westview Press, 1990.

Ziv, Avner, and Orit Gadish. "The Disinhibiting Effects of Humor: Aggressive and Affective Responses." *Humor* vol. 3, no. 3 (1990).

Laughter demolishes fear and piety before an object, before a world, making of it an object of familiar contact and thus clearing the ground for an absolutely free investigation of it. Laughter is a vital factor in laying down that prerequisite for fearlessness without which it would be impossible to approach the world realistically. As it draws an object to itself and makes it familiar, laughter delivers the object into the fearless hands of investigative experiment—both scientific and artistic—and into the hands of free experimental fantasy. Familiarization of the world through laughter and popular speech is an extremely important and indispensable step in making possible free, scientific, knowable and artistically realistic creativity in European civilization.

—M.M. Bakhtin
The Dialogic Imagination

8

The Politics of Laughter:
A Cultural Theory of Humor Preferences
(with Aaron Wildavsky)

Humor has remained a puzzle throughout the ages and as I've pointed out earlier, many of our greatest thinkers, such as Aristotle, Kant, Schopenhauer, Bergson, and Freud have speculated about what humor is and why people laugh. It still remains a subject of controversy. These thinkers and others who have worked with humor have elaborated on a large number of different theories that deal with why people laugh. But all of these theories, I suggest in my chapter on philosophical approaches to humor (and other chapters as well), can be reduced to four more or less dominant ones.

The Four Dominant Theories of Humor

Let me briefly recapitulate my discussion of the dominant theories of humor. The theory that is most widely held nowadays suggests that humor is based on incongruity, on some kind of a difference between what people expect and what they get. We can also look at incongruity in more specific terms as far as culture theory is concerned and see incongruity as suggesting some kind of a difference between what is and what is not normative.

A second important theory argues that humor involves some sense of superiority that people feel about those (people, animals, objects) they laugh at. A person slips on a banana peel and we laugh because, for a moment, we who have not lost our balance feel superior to him. From a cultural theory perspective we can extend Hobbes's notion of humor involving a sudden recognition of some kind of eminency in ourselves relative to others and say we may find this eminency not only in our persons but in our cultures.

Freud's psychoanalytic theory of humor argues that humor is tied to psychic economies and to aggression, often of a sexual nature, and usually masked. Freud wrote a book, *Jokes and Their Relation to the Unconscious,* about the subject—a book that includes, it turns out, a number of wonderful Jewish jokes in it. He pointed out that nobody made more fun of themselves than the Jews, a remark that has been distorted by some to suggest he believed that Jewish humor was masochistic.

Finally, there is a theory of humor that ties it to our cognitive abilities and the way we process information. It is connected also to semiotic theories, which deal with how people find meaning in texts and to theories that deal with how the mind resolves puzzles such as paradoxes and play frames. Gregory Bateson would be one of the more prominent cognitive theorists. It is paradox and moving in and out of play frames that generates humor for the cognitive theorists. Humor is part of play and play involves finding ways to let others know when one is playing with them that "this is play."

The semioticians would take their cue from Saussure, who explained that concepts have no meaning in themselves, but only have meaning differentially. Thus, for there to be meaning in jokes, there have to be differences, which usually take the form of polar oppositions that can be elicited from the joke.

There are numerous books by adherents of each of these four positions and some who combine them. One problem with these theories is that they don't help us deal with specific jokes or other humorous texts, except in very broad terms. Their range is too broad, also. The generalizations they make cover everyone—men and women of all socioeconomic backgrounds and other groupings (racial, ethnic, political, etc.) and in all cultures.

Four Theorists Analyze a Joke

Consider, for example, the following joke and the way representatives of our four dominant theories of humor might analyze it:

A prestigious Talmudic scholar reaches retirement and a fete is held in his honor in which he is praised from morning until night. As he leaves, late at night, a young man approaches the revered rabbi and says, "Great rabbi, your praises have been sung from morning until night. Is it enough?" The rabbi replies, "It is enough. But of my modesty, they said nothing."

Why is this joke funny? Let us consider this joke in terms of the four dominant theories of why people find things funny.

For incongruity theorists, it is the difference between what the rabbi says in response to the man's question, "It is enough," and what he says in the punch line, "but of my modesty they said nothing" (revealing his monumental ego) that generates the humor. For the superiority theorists, we laugh because we feel superior to the rabbi, who reveals, thereby diminishing himself, that he really has an enormous ego. A psychoanalytic theorist would say that we laugh at this joke because of the aggression in it, as the great rabbi is attacked; he is revealed to have an ego that is not satisfied by being praised from morning until night. The cognitive/semiotic theorists would say that the opposition between praise and modesty is at the heart of the joke. We will return to this joke after a discussion of the techniques of humor.

The cultural theory of humor preferences narrows the field and ties specific jokes and humorous texts to smaller groupings—people who belong to one of four basic cultural groups. This is a step in the right direction, in that it moves from glittering generalities about humanity to smaller cultural groupings. But before we discuss these cultural groups, another question suggests itself: Is it possible that people, regardless of their cultural groups, respond to humor because of the techniques used in these texts to generate humor?

The Techniques of Humor

The matter of the techniques of humor has been covered in the chapter on rhetoric in this book, and in more detail by myself in my book *An Anatomy of Humor* (Transaction Publishers, 1993). I suggest that there are forty-five techniques, generally used in combinations, that are found in all forms and examples of humor. These techniques deal with "what makes people laugh," and are a pragmatic typology that does not attempt to deal with why people laugh or how their cultural biases affects their responses to humor.

This rhetorical focus on techniques assumes that people in all socioeconomic classes, nationalities, and cultural groups respond, immediately and perhaps even automatically, to the various techniques of humor.

These techniques, it is implied, are psychological or more primary than "cultural." Consider the rabbi joke told above. The basic technique of humor found in the joke is revelation—the punch line reveals the true nature of the rabbi, namely, that he is somewhat of an egotist. There is also an element of reversal, as the rabbi says yes, the praises he received were adequate, *but* how come nobody mentioned his great modesty, reversing himself.

There is another approach to humor, a cultural theory of humor, that provides us with important insights into humor and its role in politics and society. A discussion of cultural theory and its application to humor follows.

Cultural Theory and Humor

Cultural theory, as elaborated by Mary Douglas, Aaron Wildavsky, and a number of others, deals with how *cultural biases* (shared values and beliefs) and *social relations* (patterns of interpersonal relations) affect our beliefs and behavior, and thus, by implication, can be used to deal with our reponses to humor. We will briefly describe cultural theory by citing one of the seminal articles on the subject, Mary Douglas's "Cultural Bias," written originally in 1978 and reprinted in her book *In the Active Voice*. In this article she writes:

> The reason for focusing upon the social context...is that each pattern of rewards and punishments moulds the individual's behaviour. He will fail to make any sense of his surroundings unless he can find some principles to guide him to behave in the sanctioned ways and be used for judging others and justifying himself to others. This is a social-accounting approach to culture; it selects out of the total cultural field those beliefs and values which are derivable as justifications for action and which I regard as constituting an implicit cosmology.

> Having divided experience into social context and cosmology, the next step is set a full array of possible social structures. A start for this will be to construct (yes, I mean construct, fabricate, think up, invent) two dimensions. One clue to finding a relevant pair of dimensions is to follow the polarizing of sociological thought between individualism and group behavior. Instead of plumping for one or the other, as has been the usual form, the procedure I am advocating is to show both, always present as possibilities. I use "grid" for a dimension of individuation, and "group" for a dimension of social incorporation. (1982, 190)

Let us see how this "grid" and "group" notion plays out by looking at an elaboration of the original figure used by Douglas. On the horizontal plane we have group boundaries and on the vertical plane we have the grid—rules and prescriptions that guide individuals. If we draw a four-celled figure, we get the following:

TABLE 8.1: Four Political Cultures

GROUP BOUNDARIES

		Weak	Strong
	Many	*Fatalistic*	*Hierarchical*
GRID RULES			
	Few	*Individualistic*	*Egalitarian*

The merit of this perspective on cultures is that it cuts across the class structure. As Douglas writes:

> It is a method of identifying cultural bias, of finding an array of beliefs locked together into relational patterns. The beliefs must be treated as part of the action, and not separated from it as in so many theories of social action. The action of social context, is placed on a two-dimensional map with moral judgements, excuses, complaints and shifts of interest reckoned as the spoken justifications by individuals of the action they feel required to take. (1982, 190)

What Douglas's grid-group conception allows is change, from one political culture to another, by individuals, as their perceptions of themselves and their possibilities are modified by their experiences. There is movement of individuals from one cultural group to another, depending upon things such as chance, bad luck, bad decisions, a lack of payoff, and that kind of thing.

According to Douglas, Wildavsky, and others who have used this grid-group perspective, there are only four ways of life that are possible: fatalist, individualistic, hierarchichal (or elitist), and egalitarian. (Wildavsky and his colleagues actually found a fifth, but it is not relevant to our concerns.) These cultures are different relative to their values and their "collective moral consciousness about man and his place in the universe" as reflected by their place in the grid-group figure, but though they are different, they all need one another.

Let me suggest some of the differences between these cultures by showing the beliefs of the four cultures as they relate to such matters as blame, envy, and a number of other matters. These attributes are impor-

TABLE 8.2: Attributes of Four Cultures

	Individualist	Hierarchical	Egalitarian	Fatalist
LEADERSHIP	each own leader	authority valid	rejects	led by others
ENVY	differences ok	not problem	big problem	no envy
BLAME	personal	deviants	system blame	fates
FAIRNESS	chance to compete	treat acc. to station	treat all equally	life not fair
WEALTH	create more, keep more	collective sacrifice	equality of condition basic	luck
RISK	opportunity to create new wealth	short run dangers	system inequality basic	luck
CONTROL	by results	process basic	consensual decisions	avoidance
OSTENTATION	okay due to need to build networks	public events only	little display	hide
EQUALITY	equal chance to compete	before law	of result basic	inequality inevitable
SCARCITY	use resources while valuable	bureaucratic control to allocate	system exploits nature	luck

tant because they can be seen in jokes and other humorous texts. For example, if we have a joke that generates its humor by system blame, we have an egalitarian joke.

This chart suggests how each of the four cultures deal with a number of phenomena such as scarcity, blame, and ostentation. In principle, members of each cultural group should respond positively to humorous texts that reflect their values and beliefs and negatively to texts that attack them. But this assumes that we respond primarily to the content of texts and not to the techniques that generate the humor found in them.

Let us return to the joke about the Talmudic scholar who was feted from morning until night. Jokes, from the cultural theory perspective, may be conceived of as involving one culture puffing itself up or putting another culture down (a subject we will deal with in more detail shortly). From this viewpoint, the joke is not about an isolated or fatalistic person, nor is it about hierarchy building up its authority. On the contrary, it is a putdown of authority showing that one of its leading members believes one thing but claims another. From the context, however, we cannot tell whether this is an egalitarian or an individualist putdown. We cannot tell whether the rabbi is simply greedy for praise, as an individualist might be, or thinks himself more worthy of praise than others, like a good hierarchical elitist. This brings out another possible classification of jokes, namely, by cultural dimensions. This joke is best described as a low-grid joke.

Problems Related to Cultural Theory and Humor

There are a number of problems we face when we try to relate cultural theory to humorous texts. For one thing, humorous texts, even seemingly simple ones like jokes, are frequently quite complicated and often use a number of different humorous techniques, in combination, to achieve their effects. This leads to an interesting question that I raised earlier: Do people respond primarily to the content of humorous texts, to the techniques that generate the humor, or to some combination of both?

Consider the following joke:

> A traveling salesman is doing business in Montana. One evening he goes to a bar and has a few drinks. A bit inebriated, he yells out "Nixon is a horse's ass!" A tough-looking cowboy sidles over to the salesman. "You'd better watch what you say," he says. "Oh, I'm sorry. I didn't realize I was in Nixon territory." "You aren't," says the cowboy. "You're in horse territory."

What are we to make of this joke? The basic techniques found in this joke are insults ("Nixon is a horse's ass"), comparisons (Nixon and the horse's ass), and reversal ("You're not in Nixon territory but in horse territory").

But which cultural group does the joke appeal to and which cultural group is ridiculed by it? The joke suggests that Nixon is not nearly as good as a horse's ass. This joke, being about a Republican president, Nixon, would appeal to a member of the Democratic party. In terms of cultural theory, the joke would appeal to egalitarians, who are critics of hierarchy and thus of Nixon, who was president, or hierarchists, who saw him as an immoral and rather gross individualist.

The fatalists, for all practical purposes, might respond to the insult and aggression in the joke, but from a cultural theory perspective they are not significant since they see life as unfair and tied to luck and chance and thus wouldn't feel envious about Nixon. In principle, however, the fatalists are the polar opposites of the individualists, who are strivers and who believe in the efficacy of personal effort and inititative.

Another interesting question suggests itself here. Are some of the forty-five techniques, described above, tied to one or another of the four cultures? That is, is there an element of cultural bias in some of the humorous techniques? Let us suggest some possible connections.

HIERARCHICAL: ridicule, dialect

INDIVIDUALIST: exaggeration, before (poor) and after (rich), imitation, eccentricity

EGALITARIAN: repartee, reversal, exposure, allusions, unmasking, insults, satire

FATALIST: absurdity, disappointment, mistakes, ignorance, accident, coincidence

These techniques, we suggest, tend to reflect or are often connected to the cultural biases of each of the groups, though we cannot argue that every situation in which we find absurdity is fatalistic or every joke involving unmasking is egalitarian.

Who Laughs at What? The Problem of Specificity

Do individuals from a particular culture, such as egalitarians, only laugh at jokes, for example, that completely reflect their cultural biases, or do they laugh at jokes because some elements in a given joke reflect them? That is, might people from all four of the cultures laugh at different parts of a particular joke or humorous text? Or, is it that people only laugh at certain jokes that are essentially congruent with their cultural biases? Or that attack other cultural groups?

We know that people, generally unconsciously, search for texts to reinforce their values and beliefs and try to avoid texts that attack their values and beliefs and create cognitive dissonance. Is it possible, however, that in some cases people laugh at jokes for the wrong reasons, as far as cultural theory is concerned, that is? Might an egalitarian, for example, laugh at a joke that reflects hierarchical values? Quite possibly, but we can assume that egalitarians laugh more heartily at jokes that reflect egalitarian beliefs and values or attack hierarchical ones.

Other questions suggest themselves. Let us take the matter of jokes as our basic form of humorous text. Do people in a given culture find jokes that support and reaffirm their cultural biases funnier and more appealing than jokes that attack other cultures? If the psychoanalytic humor theorists are correct, there's often a great deal of masked aggression in jokes. A joke that "attacks" some other cultural group tells us who we don't like, but it doesn't necessarily tell us which group is benefitting from the "attack" by having its values reaffirmed, or whether there are a number of cultural groups that get psychic payoff from a given joke or humorous text. We have dealt with this matter to a degree by showing that in some jokes we have low-grid or strong group connections.

Let us examine another joke from the cultural perspective, to show how it is useful in understanding jokes and other humorous texts.

The scene is set in the world's richest synagogue and the protagonists are the world's best rabbi and the world's finest cantor, as well as the shammes, the non-Jew who looks after the synagogue. After the glorious Yom Kippur service the three gather in the rabbi's office. The rabbi in the world's richest synagogue says to the world's best cantor that he has sung the Kol Nidre better than it has ever been sung before. In all modesty, the greatest cantor in the world says that his singing wasn't bad, but when he thinks of the great cantors of the past, he is really nothing. Then the cantor turns to the rabbi and says, "But rabbi, your sermon was the best that has been delivered anywhere at any time." In all due modesty, the world's greatest rabbi in the world's richest synagogue says that the sermon wasn't bad, but when he thinks of the great rabbis and great sermons of the past, he is really nothing. By this time the shammes thinks he understands how these Jews talk to each other and is determined not to be outdone. So when the rabbi and the cantor praise the shammes for having prepared the synagogue for the holiday better than it has ever been prepared before, the shammes replies, "The synagogue was prepared all right, but when I think of the great shammeses of the past, I'm really nothing." At this point, in unison, the world's greatest rabbi and the world's greatest cantor in the world's richest synagogue turn to each other and say, "Look who says he's nothing!"

Clearly, this arriviste is being put down for aspiring to a status to which he is not entitled. This is not an egalitarian joke because it is the lowest person in the social order who is being put down. It is not an individualist joke because the shammes, by his own abilities, is not able to rise in status, however good his work. It is not a fatalistic joke because the shammes tries. It is a hierarchical joke in which those, whether individualist or egalitarian, who try to climb the ladder of status by aping the manners of those above them, cannot succeed.

The fact that the synagogue is the world's richest synagogue and that the cantor is the world's greatest cantor and the rabbi is the world's best rabbi are clues that we are dealing with hierarchy and the joke appeals to hierarchical elitists. And the ironic punch line, "look who says he's nothing!" reinforces the point. The rabbi and cantor can say they are nothing because they know they are the world's greatest, but the shammes is not entitled to this false modesty.

There are a number of different humorous techniques found in this joke. First, we have the exaggeration, as we are told about the heroes of the joke: the world's richest synagogue, the world's greatest rabbi, and the world's best cantor. Then we have imitation, as the shammes learns from the rabbi and cantor and says that he, too (like them), is "nothing." There may be an element of misunderstanding on the part of the shammes, who hears the rabbi and cantor claim they are nothing and who might believe they actually mean it. The joke also involves unmasking and revelation, as it shows that the rabbi and cantor are really vain and are only pretending to be modest, like the Talmudic scholar in the other Jewish joke. Finally, there's the element of ridicule, as the rabbi and cantor attack the shammes for claiming, like them, to be a "nothing," since, unlike the rabbi and the cantor, he is not the greatest in the world.

The joke is a put-down of an individualist, the shammes, who aspires to a status to which he is not entitled. While hierarchical elitists and egalitarians are logical opposites, the hierarchists also face the problem of dealing with individualists who make claims to status. It is to the relationships that exist among the four cultures that we now turn our attention.

Natural Enemies and Natural Allies

We can make some progress in this matter of which groups laugh and benefit from jokes and why, by suggesting that there are natural allies and natural enemies among our four cultural groups. Thus, individualists (weak group, few rules), who believe in taking risks for private gain and in personal responsibility, are at the opposite end of the spectrum from fatalists (weak group, many rules), who think luck is basic and who are led by external forces. Egalitarians (strong group, few rules), who argue that equality of power relationships are basic, stress how everyone has certain needs and downplay differences among people, are polar opposites of hierarchists (strong group, many rules), who believe in stratification and blame deviants for difficulties, not, as egalitarians do, "the system."

There are also natural allies. The egalitarians ally themselves and strive to "lift up" the fatalists, who are the primary object of their concern in this regard (but not vice versa: the fatalists don't ally with the egalitarians). In the same light, the hierarchists and individualists make up "the establishment" in a given society and are natural allies, though as the great rabbi joke shows, they often are in conflict as individualists try to make claims to status that hierarchical groups do not believe are merited or do not wish to recognize. Though the groups are often in opposition, as cultural theorists continually point out, all the groups need each other. If there were no fatalists, for example, the egalitarians would have no group to use for criticizing the hierarchical elitists and the hierarchalists would have no group to "lord over."

NATURAL ENEMIES: Egalitarians and Hierarchical Elitists, Individualists and Fatalists

NATURAL ALLIES: Hierarchialists and Individualists, Egalitarians and Fatalists

Since there is movement by individuals from one cultural group to another, a given joke can reflect several different things. A joke ridiculing hierarchists can reflect the values and beliefs of a group, such as the individualists, that a person is connected with, or it could be an indicator of a potential movement by that person from his original group to a different one, such as the egalitarians.

The Principle of Selectivity

Probably the best way to deal with the enigmatic nature of humor is to argue for what we call the principle of selectivity. This suggests that while members of each of the groups may laugh at all kinds of different jokes, certain jokes—ones that speak most directly to the cultural biases of members of each of the cultural groups—would be seen as particularly funny and resonant. These jokes achieve this resonance by reaffirming the group's values and by attacking values held by other groups. Furthermore, it is quite likely that members of each of the four cultural groups seek out humorists who reflect their values.

Thus, egalitarians would like comedians and comediennes who support egalitarian beliefs and attack the establishment and ridicule various figures who are seen as members of it (such as politicians, business people, and celebrities) and if the performers are also sympathetic with fatalists, so much the better. In humor, the ridiculer of my enemy is my ally (just as with some in the Middle East who believe "the enemy of my enemy is my friend").

Let us consider the following joke:

> *A wasp is walking along the Nile when he meets a frog. "I've got to get over to the other side and I need someone to take me. Will you do it?" asks the wasp. "No," says the frog. "I'm afraid that when we're in the middle of the Nile you'll sting me and I'll die." "But that would be crazy," says the wasp, "because I'd die as well." "Okay," says the frog. The wasp hops on the frog's back and the frog starts swimming toward the other bank. When they are halfway there the wasp stings the frog. "How could you sting me like this when you'll die as well as me?" asks the frog. "You forget," says the wasp. "This is the Middle East."*

What are we to make of this joke? From a cultural theory perspective, it reflects a fatalistic position. In the Middle East, it suggests, hatreds are so strong and destroying enemies is so important that individuals feel compelled to kill their enemies, even if it means their self-destruction at the same time. The techniques used in the joke are rigidity (the wasp must kill frogs) and stereotyping ("this is the Middle East").

Mary Douglas has suggested in her article on "Jokes" that

> a joke is seen and allowed when it offers a symbolic pattern of a social pattern occurring at the same time. As I see it, all jokes are expressive of the social situations in which they occur. The one social condition necessary for a joke to be enjoyed is that the social group in which it is received should develop the formal characteristics of a "told" joke: that is, a dominant pattern of relations is challenged by another. If there is no joke in the social structure, no other joking can appear. (1975, 98)

This comment places humorous texts, in general, and jokes, in particular, in a new light. They are not just trivial amusements and entertainments but are related, in complicated ways, to politics and society and, as we have seen, to the four political cultures found in any society.

Since jokes are quite complicated, we must assume that individuals respond to the content of a given joke based on their identification with one of the cultural groups—a response based on reinforcing the values of the individual's cultural group or attacking those of other cultural groups. And they probably respond to the techniques generating humor in a given joke more or less automatically; most people are not aware of the various techniques found in humor, but have a great deal of experience reacting to texts with them, since these techniques are widespread, if not universal.

Conclusions

A cultural theory of humor preferences suggests that there are four political cultures in democratic societies—hierarchical elitists, individualists, egalitarians, and fatalists—and that members of each group respond to humorous texts on the basis of their allegiances to a particular political culture. The problem is complicated because a member of a political culture may be thinking about making a transition to a different one, so we can't be sure that a response to a joke, for example, is due to a sense of allegiance with an old or a potentially new political culture.

There is also the question of whether people respond to humor due to the techniques used in the humor or due to the social and political content in the humor, or some combination of the two. The cultural theory does help us understand how people respond to humor by narrowing the field and making it possible for us to talk about specific groups, with particular values and beliefs, rather than everyone in society, as mass society theorists do. A number of beliefs and attitudes toward phenomena such as leadership, envy, and blame were listed. Where there is system blame in a humorous work, it was suggested, we have an egalitarian text. In some cases, it was pointed out, we cannot determine which political culture would find a joke congruent with its beliefs, but it is possible to identify a joke, and humorous texts in general, as low-grid or high-grid, for example. Finally, a quote from Mary Douglas pointed out that jokes are intimately connected to the social structure. If there's no joke in the social structure, she reminds us, no other joking can occur.

References

Berger, Arthur Asa, ed. *Political Culture and Public Opinion*. New Brunswick, NJ: Transaction Publishers, 1989.

Berger, Arthur Asa. *Agitpop: Political Culture and Communication Theory*. New Brunswick, NJ: Transaction Publishers, 1990.

———. *An Anatomy of Humor.* New Brunswick, NJ: Transaction Publishers, 1993.

Douglas, Mary. *Implicit Meanings*. London: Routledge & Kegan Paul, 1975.
———. *In The Active Voice*. London: Routledge & Kegan Paul, 1982.
Thompson, Michael, Richard Ellis, and Aaron Wildavsky. *Cultural Theory*. Boulder, CO: Westview Press, 1990.

Humor, moreover, is not just a key to creativity; it is itself a creative act. Like a scientific theory, a painting, or a poem, even a lowly joke deals in novelty and originality. It rejects conventional thinking, makes use of imagination, and articulates the unheard-of. Conceived, like its more illustrious relatives, in a burst of inspiration, the humorous product too may be shaped and refined in painstaking dedication. While the common currency of laughter seems a far cry from art or science, while it may neither glorify nor explain life the better, it arises out of the same dissatisfaction with the status quo and asserts the same right to evolve new forms of thought and imagery.

—Harvey Mindess
Laughter and Liberation

9

On Mind and Mirth:
Psychology and Humor

We have just explored the way functionalist theory helps us understand the social dimensions of humor—how it functions in social settings, how people use humor for various gratifications, and that kind of thing. And we have dealt with humor and politics. Now we consider humor from a psychological perspective.

The Freudian Perspective

In this chapter I will devote a good deal of attention to the theories of Sigmund Freud, whose book *Jokes and Their Relations to the Unconscious* is a landmark study of humor. But I will also deal with work by other psychologists and psychiatrists on humor; it is a subject that has fascinated them and attracted a good deal of interest in terms of what humor is, how it works, and how it might be used for therapeutic purposes.

Freud starts his book with a survey of the literature—a discussion of theories about jokes and explanations of humor that existed prior to his book. He mentions Theodor Lipps's theory that humor involves the subjective, Kuno Fischer's idea that the comic is involved with the ugly (in one of its manifestations), and Kraepelin's belief that the comic involves the linking of incongruous ideas. Freud also mentions a number of other theories, such as the one that sees humor as involving "sense in nonsense" and another that suggests it involves the movement from bewilderment to enlightenment.

After excusing himself for an abbreviated treatment of these theories, Freud suggests that none of them is adequate. They are, he says, *"disjecta membra,"* which need to be combined into some kind of a coherent whole. They are equivalent, he adds, to a series of anecdotes about a person when what we really require is a serious biography. What is needed, Freud continues, is some kind of an organizing principle that will enable us to link everything together. He solves this problem by looking at the mind. There is, he writes, "an intimate connection between all mental happenings" so that jokes are, it turns out, susceptible to psychoanalytic investigation.

Freud then offers an example of a joke, having mentioned earlier that he would be dealing, primarily, with jokes that he thinks are funny. He mentions a character of the great German writer Heine, one Hirsch-Hyacinth, a lottery agent and extractor of corns, who boasts one day, "I sat beside Salomon Rothschild and he treated me quite as his equal—quite famillionairely" (1960, 16). Why is this a joke? asks Freud. Either because of the thought or the form, he replies, and in the Hirsch-Hyacinth joke, it is because of the form—the contraction of the two words *familiar* and *millionaire* into *famillionaire*. He offers several other examples, *anecdotage* and *alcoholidays*.

After discussing jokes formed by *condensation* (and the forming of compound words) he moves on to his second major category of jokes, multiple-use jokes, created by *condensation with modification,* or as Freud puts it, "condensation with substitute formation." In these jokes a word is used in a number of different ways, as in the following joke:

> *An Italian lady is said to have revenged herself for a tactless remark of the first Napoleon's with a joke having the same double use of a word. At a court ball, Napoleon said to her, pointing to her fellow countrymen, "Tutti gli Italiani danzano si male." To which she made the quick repartee: "Non tutti, ma buona parte."* (1960, 31)

Napoleon had said that all (tutti) the Italians dance poorly, to which she replied, playing on Buonaparte's name, not all (tutti) but a good many (buona parte) of them do.

The third basic category of jokes that Freud discusses are based on *double meanings,* which involves forms, such as a word that is both a name and a thing, playing upon words, and double entendres. Freud cites Shakespeare's *Henry IV,* Part II as an example of the first case, where we find the line "Discharge thyself of our company, Pistol" (1960, 36). For a play on words he tells the following joke:

A doctor, as he came away from a lady's bedside, said to her husband with a shake of his head, "I don't like her looks." "I've not liked her looks for a long time," the husband hastened to agree. (1960, 37)

As an example of a double entendre, Freud mentions a statement of Napoleon III upon seizing the property of the House of Orleans, "C'est le premier vol de l'aigle," which means either "this is the first *flight* of the eagle" or "this is the first *theft* of the eagle." *Vol* means either flight or theft in French.

All of these jokes, Freud points out, have something in common—the tendency toward compression. These jokes all involve some kind of an "economy," we might say, but that does not mean that the reverse is true, that all economy has a joke-like quality to it. Freud then investigates other forms of jokes that depend on a variety of techniques. Since there are a number of these techniques and the matter is relatively complex, I will simplify things by adopting the following format: I will name the technique, explain how it functions (its methods), and provide an example or two by way of illustration. All of the following material, except where specifically noted, is taken from Freud. I have modified some of the explanations and some of the jokes, many of which, it should be pointed out, are Jewish jokes.

Displacement Jokes

Method: Diverts the train of thought onto a topic other than the opening one; displacement of psychical emphasis; diversion of meaning.
Example:

Two Jews met in the neighborhood of the bath-house. "Have you taken a bath?" asks one of them. "What," replies the other, "is one of them missing?"

In this example, the displacement from *bath* to *taken* is the basis of the joke. This joke is based on the technique of misunderstanding. The first Jew asks his friend whether he's had a bath; the second Jew interprets the "taken" to mean that a bath is missing.
Example:

An impoverished man borrowed twenty-five florins from a prosperous benefactor, with much talk about how urgently the money was needed—to pay the rent, to feed starving children, and so on. A short while later the benefactor sees the

impoverished man at the local restaurant with a plate of salmon and mayon-
naise in front of him. "What?" cries the benefactor. "You borrowed money
from me and then you use it to eat salmon and mayonnaise? Is that what you've
used the money for?" "I don't understand you," replied the impoverished man.
"If I haven't any money I can't eat salmon and mayonnaise and if I have money
I mustn't eat salmon and mayonnaise. Well, then, when am I to eat salmon and
mayonnaise?"

In this joke, the man who borrowed the money displaced the questioner's
intention from the logical one (how come a poor man who needs money
eats expensive delicacies) to a mock logical one (when *am* I to eat salmon
and mayonnaise?).

Characterizing Joke

Method: Shows the character of people by examples of their actions.
Example:

A schadken (marriage broker) assures a suitor that the father of the woman he's
about to marry is dead. After the marriage it turns out that the bride's father is
alive and serving a sentence in prison. The groom protests to the schadken, who
replies "Well, what did I tell you. You surely don't call that living?"

Here the broker shows his mendacious impudence. A person in prison is
alive, true, but you can't call that "living." The joke also mocks the
"sacredness" of marriage by exposing the calculating that goes on before many weddings take place.

Nonsense Jokes

Method: Uses nonsense to demonstrate other nonsense and how absurd people often are.
Example:

First person: *"Never to be born would be the best thing for mortal man."*
Second person: *"But this happens to scarcely one person in a hundred thousand."*

Here the stupidity of the reply uncovers the inanity of the original statement, which, at first glance, appears to be profound. If you aren't born
you aren't mortal, so the question of what would be best for you is irrel-
evant. And the idea that hardly one in a hundred thousand people is not
born is absurd.

Appearance of Logic

Method: A narrative seems to be logical but when examined more closely is found to be based on faulty reasoning.
Example:

A gentleman entered a pastry cook's shop and ordered a cake. But soon he brought it back and asked for a drink instead. He drank it and began to leave without paying for his drink. The proprietor detained him. "You've not paid for the drink." "But I gave you the cake for it." "But you didn't pay for that, either." "But I hadn't eaten it."

Here the customer creates a situation that seems logical but that, in reality, is illogical. The two processes, paying for the cake and paying for the drink, are independent of each other and you cannot use a cake that you didn't buy and didn't eat to pay for a drink that you consumed.

Unification (Repartee)

Method: New and unexpected unities or combinations are established or ideas are related to one another mutually or with reference to a common third element.
Example:

A royal person was making a tour through his provinces and noticed a man in a crowd who bore a remarkable resemblance to his own exalted personage. He beckoned to the man in the crowd and asked "Was your mother at one time in service in the palace?" "No," replied the man, "but my father was!"

Repartee consists in the defense going to meet the aggression and in turning the tables on someone, that is, establishing an unexpected unity between an attack and a counterattack. In the joke, the royal personage's question suggested that the subject's mother had been impregnated while in service in the court. The subject turns the tables and suggests that it was the royal personage's mother.

Representation by Opposite (Irony) or Similarity

Method: We mean the opposite of what we say (often by overstatement or a tone in our voice) or we make an unflattering association (an allusion).
Example:

This lady resembles the Venus of Milo in many respects: she, too, is extraordinarily old, like her she has no teeth, and there are white patches on the yellowish surface of her body.

In the joke a woman is compared to the Venus de Milo, but not in a flattering way as might be expected, but in the opposite way, connecting the woman to the age of the statue and its decrepit condition.

Freud lists other subcategories of jokes and admits that some techniques of jokes may have escaped him, though he claims that he had dealt with the most common methods of jokes . He finds, also, that there is a basic similarity between jokes and the three basic aspects of dreams : transformation, condensation, and displacement. In transformation, latent thoughts are transformed into manifest ones; in condensation, material is compressed greatly; and in displacement, items that are on the periphery of our consciousness become of central concern and gain a good deal of intensity, and vice versa.

On the Psychological Mechanisms Involved in Jokes

This leads Freud to make a hypothesis about jokes. In jokes, Freud writes: "*[A] preconscious thought is given over for a moment to unconscious revision and the outcome of this is at once grasped by conscious perception*" (1960, 166). There is, in jokes, a "sudden release of intellectual tension" (1960, 167) that eventuates in the joke, which, all of a sudden, appears and causes pleasure.

Freud makes numerous classifications and distinctions that are important. First, he distinguishes between *innocent* jokes, in which the joke is an end in itself, and *tendentious* jokes, which have a purpose and often have a social dimension. The basic purposes of tendentious jokes for Freud are hostility and obscenity, but there are also other kinds of tendentious jokes that are cynical, critical, blasphemous (and ridicule people and institutions), or skeptical (and raise the problem of the certainty of knowledge and the meaning of truth).

Obscene jokes, which Freud calls "smut," represent an attempt at seduction. They involve "the intentional bringing into prominence of sexual facts and relations by speech" (1960, 97), are tied to exposure and exhibitionism, and function by arousing sexual excitement. Freud suggests that tendentious jokes involve three parties: the person telling the joke (who gains pleasure in telling it), the listener (who enjoys hearing the joke), and the object of the joke. Jokes create pleasure, Freud adds, by easing repression:

> They make possible the satisfaction of an instinct (whether lustful or hostile) in face of an obstacle that stands in its way. They circumvent this obstacle and in that way draw pleasure from a source which the obstacle has made inaccessible. The obstacle standing in the way is in reality nothing other than women's incapacity to tolerate undisguised sexuality, an incapacity correspondingly increased with a rise in income and social level. (1960, 101)

Tendentious jokes, then, are a way of getting around repressions and some of the discontents of civilization. These jokes create pleasure because they permit an economy in psychical expenditure in surmounting inhibitions. Innocent jokes create pleasure by their coupling of unlikely things and the ease with which they permit the discovery of something familiar. Nonsense jokes are enjoyable because they allow us to regress and play around with sounds and babble.

Freud is also interested in the social dimensions of jokes and devotes a chapter to that topic. Freud believes that among the basic motivations of telling jokes are: to show one's cleverness and, in smutty jokes, to "display" oneself (so to speak). Jokes are social and need an audience, Freud says, and they tend to unite their listeners. He writes: "[E]very joke calls for a public of its own and laughing at the same jokes is evidence of far-reaching psychical conformity" (1960, 151). People laugh at jokes, Freud suggests (and this may be an answer to our question of why people who "read" jokes differently laugh at the same time at humorous texts) when they are in psychic accord and possess the same inhibitions as the joke teller and when they have no other way of directing their liberated energy. Jokes, then, are a key to our inhibitions and the subjects about which we have strong interests and feelings.

Freud's Synthesis

Freud's book and a later article, *Humour,* written in 1928, are extremely complex and must be read to be fully appreciated. He distinguishes, for example, between jokes, the comic, and humor in general. His theory, which suggests that there are unconscious elements in humor and that much of it involves masked aggression, remains one of the dominant explanations of why people laugh. The concluding paragraph of *Jokes and Their Relation to the Unconscious* summarizes his findings and suggests that some kind of an economy is behind our enjoyment of jokes, the comic, and humor:

> We are now at the end of our task, having reduced the mechanism of humorous pleasure to a formula analogous to those for comic pleasure and for jokes. The pleasure in jokes has seemed to arise from an economy of expenditure upon inhibition, the pleasure in the comic from an economy in expenditure upon ideation (upon cathexis) and the pleasure in humour from an economy of expenditure upon feeling. In all three modes of working of our mental apparatus the pleasure is derived from an economy. All three are agreed in representing methods of regaining from mental activity a pleasure which has in fact been lost through the development of that activity. (1960, 235–36)

In the final analysis, we attempt to return to the state of euphoria of our childhood when, Freud tells us, we didn't know about the comic, we had developed to a level in which we could make jokes, and we had no need of humor to make us happy.

Freud's theory suggests that humor is tied to various psychological drives we feel (aggression and sex), to the pleasure we get in certain kinds of mental activity associated with humor, and to economies and regressions (in the service of the ego) we experience when exposed to humor. It is, perhaps, somewhat reductionistic, but he does focus our attention, directly, on the role the psyche and unconscious play in humor and in the social dimensions of humor.

In *Motivation in Humor,* a collection of articles on humor by psychologists, Jacob Levine suggests that there are three models commonly used to explain the motivational sources of humor, and psychoanalytic theory is one of them. The other two are cognitive-perceptual theories and drive-reduction theories of humor.

Cognitive-Perceptual Theories of Humor

What Levine calls cognitive-perceptual theories focus on getting the point of a joke, on understanding the symbolic and semantic aspects of the humor. As he writes about cognitive-perceptual theories:

> "Getting the joke" is the real source of pleasure in humor. In comprehending the point of a joke, we are able to master the symbolic properties of the event with the multiple meanings and the figurative and allegorical allusions.... The sudden discovery achieved by the reshuffling of the symbols and meanings into a surprisingly new relationship is the source of the gratification. (1969, 4)

Levine also discusses the work of theorists who use the concept of "schemas" to understand the way the human mind works and discusses work by psychologists on schemas, which are defined as "the representation of an external pattern" (1969, 5).

A related cognitive-perceptual approach, as exemplified by the work of Gregory Bateson and William Fry on paradoxes and metacommunication, was discussed in the chapter on communication and humor. For these authors, the unexpected resolution of a series of paradoxes, climaxed by a punch line, is the source of pleasure in humor.

Drive-Reduction Theories of Humor

The third of Levine's basic theories is based on stimulus-response learning and drive reduction and has led, he suggests, to much interesting experimental research on humor. The drive-reduction theory, in essence, suggests that humor generates pleasure in people by satisfying and therefore reducing the primary drives of sex and aggression.

He cites the work of D. E. Berlyne, who uses a drive-reduction model to explain humor (and other activities such as play, curiosity, and exploration). Berlyne argues that humor is caused by an "arousal jag" that stems from an experience of threat, uncertainty, discomfort, unfamiliarity, and so on that is followed by "some factor that signifies safety, readjustment, clarification, or release" (1969, 6). Berlyne believes, Levine adds, that arousal in humor is a neurophysiological event and not a psychological state, and is a response by the nervous system to something demanding energetic action.

This view, Levine points out, is very similar to Kant's definition of humor as "an affection arising from a strained expectation being suddenly reduced to nothing." Many experimental scientists have done research on humor, assuming that our enjoyment of humor can be explained in learning theory terms, since humor allegedly reduces aggressive or sexual drives. This theory is similar to Freud's except that it focuses on a stimulus and a response, and leaves out the mediating process that Freud believes exists between a stimulus and a response.

Experimental approaches to humor have been dominated, Levine says, by two basic approaches. The first takes individuals who have a high degree of some personality trait, such as aggressiveness, and compares their humor preferences with individuals having a small degree of that personality trait. The second approach involves experimentally arousing subjects, either sexually or by making them angry, and then comparing their humor preferences with subjects who have not been aroused.

In both of these approaches, we should notice, the focus is not on humor, per se, but on the way humor relates to some psychological state such as aggressiveness or sexual arousal. Humor is used to find out something about people rather than people being used to find out something about humor.

Humor and Psychological Development

Harvey Mindess, a psychologist who has written a good deal about humor, deals with development and humor. He takes a cue from Freud, who offered some speculations about how our sense of humor evolves as we get older, and from Shakespeare, who wrote about the eight stages of man. Mindess offers a rough guide to the way our physical and psychological development shapes our sense of humor. This perspective, he writes, "strikes to the core of our sense of humor's role in our lives" (1987, 83).

He offers a list of kinds of humor that, more or less, show how the kind of humor we like correlates, approximately, to our development. This list follows:

1. Nonsense and wordplay
2. Comic relief
   A. ribaldry
   B. scatology
   C. sick humor
   D. degrading or hostile (including ethnic) humor
3. Social Satire
4. Philosophical humor or comic vision
5. Self-directed humor
6. Creation, destruction and re-creation in the structure of humor.

Mindess doesn't claim, explicitly, that this list mirrors our development, and in some cases, such as self-directed humor, he points out that children can laugh at themselves as well as adults. But his article has a chronological cast to it, and starts with nonsense and wordplay, which, he suggests, are among the earliest forms of humor that humans like.

He recounts a moron joke and a "knock knock" joke as examples:

Q. *Why did the moron toss his watch out the window?*
A. *He wanted to see time fly.*

Knock knock.
Who's there?
Dwayne.
Dwayne who?
Dwayne the bathtub. I'm dwowning.

I will not offer examples of humor or jokes that exemplify each of his categories. But I would like to say something about his last category, which he considers extremely important.

He explains his reasoning as follows:

> Humor provides us with recreation, which is actually re-creation—a restructuring of our thoughts and feelings, our attitudes toward ourselves and our perception of the world....In pursuing an analysis of humor, we have come across a pattern that seems fundamental to existence. A great impersonal force appears to be at work, a force that destroys old patterns of being in the creation of new ones, and the structure of humor reflects the working of this force. (Mindness, 1987, 94)

This force, incidentally, is a liberating one—a force that enables us to escape from rigidity, conformity, fear, and overseriousness. These subjects are discussed in greater detail in his book *Laughter and Liberation,* which also has some wonderful jokes in it.

Mindess sums up his article by suggesting it reveals three important patterns. One involves the movement from interpreting laughter as a relief of tension to recognizing laughter as a sign of an enhanced or expanded understanding. A second involves the change from taking ourselves too seriously to "lightening up" and laughing at ourselves. The third is based on the structure of humor itself, and not the content of humor; here Mindess is talking about a pattern of creation, destruction, and recreation (and re-creation) found in humor and which, he suggests, may be the basis of humor. This pattern, it is interesting to note, is similar to one elaborated on in a classic work by Melanie Klein, *Love, Hate and Reparation.*

Humor and Therapy

There is a good deal of disagreement among therapists about the use of humor in therapy. Lawrence Kubie wrote an article in the *American Journal of Psychiatry* in 1971 on "The Destructive Potential of Humor in Psychotherapy," cautioning against the use of humor by therapists. Humor could be used, Kubie wrote, to disparage patients, to subject them to ridicule, and also to serve as a vehicle for a therapist's narcissistic self-satisfaction.

But Kubie was referring to hostile or aggressive humor, and not to gentle, tolerant humor. Kubie recognized this limitation, as a matter of fact, and wrote, at the end of his paper: "The critical difference is between smiling or laughing *with* someone (which rarely does harm) or smiling or laughing *at* them" (1971, 865). Another problem connected with using humor in therapeutic situations is that humor can also expose various problems and difficulties that therapists have. There is also the matter of patients using humor defensively to justify their behavior and obstruct the therapeutic process. Still, Kubie's suggestion that humor never be used therapy is simplistic and deprives patients of valuable experiences they may have if humor is used carefully and intelligently.

In his paper "Points of Correspondence between Humor and Psychotherapy" (delivered at the Eighty-Ninth Annual Convention of the American Psychological Association, 28 August 1981), Joseph Richman argues that humor can be an effective agent in therapy if used correctly. He writes (1981, 8):

> Humor can serve as an effective ice breaker for the relief of tension....Such humor can also be valuable during critical moments in therapy, but with some important provisos: The humor must be appropriate to the situation and the content being discussed; the timing must be right; and the humor must not be used defensively or to avoid an issue.

In his article Richmond describes a number of different clinical examples in which humor has been an effective therapeutic instrument. He discusses such matters as the use of humor in situational crises, humor as a form of self-help, humor in psychoanalysis, humor in behavior therapy, and humor in existential therapy.

He concludes by suggesting that there are basic similarities between humor and therapy: they both involve the ability to see oneself and one's situation in new and different terms, they both expose lies and folly, they both reveal often unpalatable truths, they both help achieve a mastery of drives, and they both foster individual integration and social harmony.

The Importance of Humorous Techniques in Self-Therapy

In an essay I wrote on the comics, "Funnies are Good for Us: Healthful Benefits of Humorous Comic Strips" (*The World & I,* May 1992) I suggested that it was the techniques used by the humorists that are instrumental, not the subjects they deal with. I argued that humor helps us on four levels: the biological, the intrapsychic, the interpersonal, and the social.

At every level, it was the humorous techniques, used to generate laughter (or a smile), that played the most important role. As I pointed out, in looking over joke books I found that the same joke was often told with different characters. In one version, for example, the joke was about a general, in another the president of a university, and in a third, a king. It wasn't the "subject" that was crucial in the joke, but the techniques (ridicule, insult, exaggeration, etc.). These jokes, and humorous comic strips, serve a therapeutic function.

They help us learn not to take ourselves too seriously, they point out how absurd people often are, they help us deal with anxieties we have about social and political events, and they do a number of other things for us. So reading the funnies (a misnomer because a number of comic strips aren't humorous) and exposure to humor of all kinds, in cartoons, in the routines of stand-up comedians, in situation comedies and film comedies, does a good deal for us, even though we may not necessarily be aware of what humor does for us or how it helps us.

Humor about Psychiatrists and Therapists

In my chapter on communication, I told a classic joke about a child psychiatrist who is outwitted by two children—one a died-in-the-wool pessimist and the other a born optimist. I also suggested that we tend to see psychiatrists as powerful, though often absurd, figures and feel a considerable amount of anxiety about them. To deal with this anxiety we diminish them by calling them "shrinks," alluding to the practices of certain head hunters who decapitate their victims and preserve their heads. We also make jokes to show that they are generally just as crazy, neurotic, compulsive, whatever, as their patients or that frequently they don't listen to their patients.

Let me offer a sampling of psychiatrist/therapist jokes now.
Joke 1:

A young psychiatrist is going home at 5:00 P.M., after a hard day with his patients. His shirt is rumpled, and he's exhausted. On the elevator he notices an older psychiatrist, with an office on the same floor, who looks fresh and shows no signs of fatigue at all. "How do you do it?" asks the young psychiatrist. "I'm absolutely exhausted after a day of listening to my patients talk about their problems. But you don't seem to be tired at all." "Who listens!" replies the older psychiatrist.

This joke deals with the fear that many people in therapy have that their therapists aren't really listening to them, but are, more or less, merely going through the motions. The older psychiatrist is revealing something important and the joke is based on the technique of revelation.

Joke 2:

A psychiatrist is describing a case he has to a colleague. "I have this patient who has a multiple personality problem. He thinks he's two people. It's really wonderful having that kind of patient to deal with." "How so?" asks the second psychiatrist. The first replies, "They both pay!"

This joke is based on the technique of absurdity: a patient has two identities and each pays the psychiatrist. It also uses the technique of exposure to show the mercenary nature of psychiatrists, who "really" are interested in money, many patients feel, and not in helping them with their difficulties.

Joke 3:

After a number of years of treating a patient, his psychiatrist decides it is time to terminate the treatment. The patient is very anxious so the psychiatrist agrees to let the patient call him on an emergency basis. The next morning, at 6:00 A.M. the psychiatrist gets a call from the patient. "I dreamed you were my mother," says the patient.

"So...then what happened?"
"I made myself some breakfast to calm my nerves."
"What did you make?"
"A cup of coffee."
"A cup of coffee? You call that a breakfast?"

This joke is based on the technique of revelation. The psychiatrist unconsciously "assumes" the role of a mother and chastises the man for not making a healthy breakfast, the way mothers often do. The patient has dreamed the psychiatrist is his mother, the joke reveals, because he has been treating the patient like a mother.

Joke 4:

A lady visits a psychiatrist to discuss a problem her husband has. "It's incredible," she says. "My husband thinks he's a horse. He lives in a stable, walks on all fours and even eats hay. What should I do? Can you cure him, doctor?"

"Yes," I think I can, says the psychiatrist, "but this is a very difficult case and the treatment will be very expensive."

"That's no problem," says the wife. "You see, he's already won two races."

In this joke, we find another absurd situation: a man thinks he's a horse and acts like one. But the punch line adds to the absurdity, for not only does he act like a horse, he's won two races. The joke deals with the triumph of absurdity over rationality and logic. The joke isn't so much about psychiatrists as it is about the absurd nature of life and the irrational behavior of people. We learn from this joke that as crazy as we may think we are, there are people who are a lot crazier.

Conclusions

Our minds, those "ghosts" in the "machines" of our bodies, play a vital role in our responses to humor, and in particular, as Freud pointed out, the unconscious and preconscious elements in our minds. Even the psychologists who deal with drive reductions and stimulus-response experiments tend to focus on aggression and sexual arousal, areas that Freud indicated were of major importance in understanding humor, jokes, the comic, and related matters.

Humor, we have seen, has therapeutic value in itself, it has values in the therapeutic process, and, as I have argued, it is the techniques used to generate humor—techniques such as exaggeration, absurdity, revelation, and misunderstanding—that do the work, so to speak, of helping us with our psychological difficulties.

Jokes offer us a world of hyperfixated monomaniacs, of zanies, of people who think they are horses (and win races, to boot), and of people with multiple identities (each of which pays the psychiatrist). We can see, in these comic characters, that nobody is perfect, that everyone has his or her hang-ups, and that we frequently misunderstand one another (and that sometimes this misunderstanding is good). Thus, we learn to be easier on ourselves and others and that represents a giant step we take toward escaping from anxieties and inhibitions and achieving mental health.

We are now ready to turn to our next chapter, which deals not with some disciplinary or metadisciplinary approach to humor, but with an important kind of humor—visual humor. In analyzing visual humor, we can use the information we have learned and the insights we have gained from the various disciplinary approaches that have been discussed to deal with cartoons, comic strips, and other forms of visual humor such as optical illusions and visual puns.

References

Freud, Sigmund. *Jokes and Their Relation to the Unconscious.* New York: Norton, 1963.

Kubie, Lawrence, "The Destructive Potential of Humor in Psychotherapy." In *A Celebration of Laughter,* edited by Werner Mendel. Los Angeles: Mara Books, 1970.

Levine, Jacob, ed. *Motivation in Humor.* New York: Atherton, 1969.

Mindess, Harvey. "The Panorama of Humor and the Meaning of Life." *American Behavioral Scientist,* vol. 30, no. 3 (January/February 1987).

———. *Laughter and Liberation.* Los Angeles: Nash Publishing, 1971.

The most exemplary of modern comedians, Charlie Chaplin, managed to incorporate an agon—nay, virtually a class-struggle—within his fragile, shabby-genteel figure: the threadbare little tramp with the minute moustache and the mincing manners, crowned by a bowler hat and armed with a walking-stick, politely smiling, fastidiously tipping his hat, and waddling away into the sunset. Let us not forget that he began his picaresque career as a heavy English swell, a drunken music-hall toff. This dualism would be grandly externalized in The Great Dictator, *wherein he plays the dual role of the* eiron, *the little Jewish barber, and the* alazon, *Hynker/Hitler. To cite some early titles, the contrast he sustained was between* The Tramp *or* A Dog's Life, *on the one hand, and* Easy Street *or* The Idle Class *on the other—in short, between rags and riches. He embodied survival, if not triumph, for life's waifs and strays, for all the fall guys, sad sacks, and lame ducks who ever tried to dodge a cop.*

> —Harry Levin
> *Playboys & Killjoys: An Essay on the Theory & Practice of Comedy*

10

Seeing Laughter:
Visual Aspects of Humor

Because so much humor is verbal—jokes told by our friends, routines by stand-up comics, gags in situation comedies, and so on—we tend to forget that visual phenomena are frequently used to generate humor, often in conjunction with written or spoken humor. Think, for example, of the way stand-up comics use facial expression and body language as part of their routines, or of the expressions on the faces of comic strip and cartoon characters. I dealt with certain elements of this phenomenon in my discussion of clowns; now I would like to focus attention on graphic media such as cartoons and comic strips.

Visual Aspects of Humorous Cartoons

Cartoons are generally defined as drawings, in one frame (though sometimes we see cartoons with a number of different scenes in them), with characters who keep changing, that are meant to be funny. Dialogue, constituting a gag line, generally is not in balloons but underneath the frame. In most cartoons the humor is created by the gag line, but it has to fit in with the "look" of the characters in the cartoon. That is, the characters in a given cartoon have to look like the kind of people who would make the statements found in the gag lines and the humor is connected to the ability of the cartoonist to capture (visually) certain types of characters and create the kind of statements they might make, or fit in with some kind of a caption, if the gag line is not based on dialogue.

Consider Gary Larson's *The Far Side,* one of the most original and brilliant American cartoons. Larson's characters are all funny looking, with bulbous bodies, big noses, and stupid expressions on their faces and these visual characteristics reinforce Larson's bizarre and offbeat humor. He also uses weird-looking bugs, animals, and extraterrestrials in his strip. None of his characters continue on from one cartoon to the next, but many of his types do: professors, explorers, aliens, and so on.

In *The New Yorker,* which carries a large number of cartoons every week, there are a variety of cartoonists, each of whom has a distinctive line and style and type of character. Most cartoonists do not think up their own gags, but buy them from gag writers. But only certain gags are congruent with the style of a given cartoonist and his or her "typical" characters. Charles Addams is a good example. He is associated with a cast of weird characters and with unnatural and zany phenomena: ski tracks in the snow that go on both sides of a tree, a moose driving a car with a hunter tied to the fender (the technique of reversal), and that kind of thing.

In many cartoons there is no gag line underneath the cartoon; the cartoon shows a scene that is, in itself, humorous. That is, the drawing reveals something about human nature, shows how odd and zany some people are, and, by doing so, is seen as "funny." These cartoons without gag lines make use, one way or another, of the various techniques of humor, but they do so in a visual and nonverbal way.

There's a wonderful cartoon from *Punch* by Anton that shows everyone but one person in an audience smiling as a hero is about to rescue a damsel in distress from a villain. That one person who is not smiling is, we see from his clothes and hairstyle, a villain himself. Another example from *Punch,* by Sprod, shows a statue of a man holding a scroll in his left hand and reaching out with his right hand. A dog is shown on its hind legs, "begging." It has mistaken the pose of the statue and assumes the man is alive and is about to give it something to eat.

In another nonverbal *Punch* cartoon by J. W. Taylor we see a man standing by a tree and in a balloon we see the head of a young woman whom he is obviously waiting for. In the next drawing we see him looking at his watch, indicating that she's late and that time is passing. The drawing of the woman is getting fainter. In the third drawing the woman's head has changed so it looks like a head but it also might be a mug of beer. And in the fourth drawing, the head has become a mug of beer and the man is walking off to get a beer (having, we assume, been stood up by his date or got tired of waiting for her).

This cartoon shows the power of visual phenomena to generate humor. It is the head of the woman and the transformations it undergoes as the man thinks about her that generates the humor. This gag could not be expressed as well verbally, for the cartoon depends on readers actually seeing the transformations of the head; that is what creates the humor. The same applies to the dog begging for food from the statue. It works as a drawing but would not work as a joke. The drawings can show facial expressions, can show body language, can ridicule conventions, popular taste, fads and that kind of thing.

A classic cartoon from *The New Yorker* shows an elderly woman dressed in a *Playboy* Club bunny outfit, waiting for her husband with a tray and a drink. It is the drawing and the concept that are so amusing, and this could not be told as a joke, for we have to see the old woman in her bunny costume to get the proper effect. I should point out that in many cases it is the concept in a purely visual cartoon that is important and the visual expression of that concept may be thought of as important but not as crucial to the humor as the idea itself.

Humorous Comic Strips

The term *comics* is really a misnomer, because many of our classic comic strips, such as *Dick Tracy, Little Orphan Annie, Buck Rogers,* and many contemporary comics are not meant to be funny. But historically a large number of the comics were humorous. In the early days, we had remarkable comic strips such as *The Yellow Kid* (considered our first comic strip, though it might not technically qualify as a comic strip), *The Katzenjammer Kids, Mutt and Jeff, Krazy Kat, Blondie, Pogo,* and *Li'l Abner,* just to name some of the more prominent ones. Of course, now we have *Peanuts, Doonesbury, Calvin and Hobbes* (and we still have *Blondie*), and a number of newer comic-strip artists, such as Robert Crumb, Gary Panter, Victoria Roberts, and Matt Groening as well.

As M. Thomas Inge writes in *Comics as Culture*: "What would prove to be an abiding presence in the comic strip was the American sense of humor. Most of the popular titles that came in the wake of the Kid for three decades were primarily characterized by humor and fantasy" (1990, 5). He lists a number of comics such as *Happy Hooligan, Maude the Mule, Buster Brown,* and *Little Nemo;* one could go on and on here.

Technically speaking, comic strips are understood to have the following attributes: many frames, continuing characters, and dialogue in balloons. Unlike cartoons, in which the characters change from day to day (though the same type of character may be found in the cartoons, they are not the same characters, per se), comic strips keep their characters—sometimes for fifty or sixty years, as a matter of fact.

There are two kinds of humorous comic strips: the gag strip, which has some kind of a funny resolution every day, and the continuing strip, which can last weeks and months, and relies on zany personalities and narrative complications to amuse readers. In comic strips the characters sometimes evolve visually as the artist develops his or her style. *Peanuts* is a case in point. Schulz's first drawings were relatively crude, but after years and years of drawing his characters, his line has become quite fluid and his characters look somewhat different from their earliest incarnations.

In some cases, it is hard to say whether what we have is a cartoon or a strip. Is *Dennis the Menace,* which has a continuing character but is generally drawn in one frame, a cartoon or a comic strip? Or is *Doonesbury* really a political cartoon in comic strip format? The lines are somewhat fuzzy now, as some artists cross the line between the comic strips and political cartoons from time to time.

Krazy Kat: Comic Strip or Work of Elite Art?

Krazy Kat, which some critics believe to be the greatest comic strip ever to appear in America, was extremely original, and almost surrealistic in its use of language and its spatiality. Inge sees the strip as an example of Dada art and comments on the way the strip disorients readers of the strip "through the transmutation of figures, landscape, and objects," which was, he suggests, a practice of Dadaists and Surrealists. Herriman's use of language, essentially for the pleasure he got in playing with the sound and the meanings of words, reminds Inge of the work of James Joyce, the great modernist writer. At Herriman's best, Inge adds, "his language becomes pure poetry, just as his imagery becomes pure art" (1990, 49).

The humor in *Krazy Kat* stems from a bizarre triangle in which a cat, Krazy Kat, is in love with a mouse, Ignatz, who spends more than thirty years throwing a brick at her—which she mistakenly takes as a sign of love. (There is a question of whether Krazy is actually a female; let us assume that she is.) The third character in the triangle is a policeman, Offissa Pupp, who loves Krazy Kat and spends his time trying to protect her from being hit by one of Ignatz's bricks. When Pupp catches Ignatz heaving a brick, Pupp jails him. (For a more detailed analysis of the strip, see Inge's book, *Comics as Culture,* and my book *The Comic-Stripped American.* Both books devote a chapter to *Krazy Kat.*)

Krazy Kat was probably the most avant-garde, surrealistic strip, but there have been numerous other strips that were experimental and adventurous. Currently, the most interesting new strip, in my opinion, is *Calvin and Hobbes,* which details the adventure of a mischievous little boy, Calvin, and his toy tiger, Hobbes. It is a gag strip, and has some kind of a funny resolution to it each day. Part of the humor of comic strips, however, comes from the way we learn more and more about the characters as we follow them over the years. Thus, we seem to "know" them in what could be described as a parasocial relationship and we can thus derive more enjoyment from them as the years go by. So, as we get to know Calvin and his tiger Hobbes, we get a bigger kick out of their exploits, appreciate Calvin's imagination all the more, and learn about all kinds of things (since there is at times a didactic streak to the strip—as in the September 1992 strips that dealt with the nature of photography).

Humorous Political Cartoons

Not all political cartoons are humorous; some are grim and even terrifying. But humor is one of the main techniques political cartoonists use in drawing the attention of their readers to various aspects of their social and political world. One of the most important humorous techniques political cartoonists use is caricature, which is understood to be a drawing that resembles a particular individual but takes liberties with his or her features. The fact that a person's resemblance is "captured" but that various aspects of the person's features are exaggerated is, in itself, humorous. Exaggeration is one of the more important techniques of humor.

A classic French political cartoon of 17 January 1831, "The Pears" by Philipon, appeared in the magazine *Le Charivari* (figure 10.1). The cartoon plays with the face of King Louis-Phillipe (whose face was pearlike in shape) and in four images turns him into a pear. Censors eventually forbade artists to draw any pearlike figure in their cartoons. In an essay "International Wit and Humor as Expressed in Caricature" Arthur Bartlett Maurice writes:

> The Revolution of 1830 brought political caricature back into popularity, and with the ripening genius of Daumier and Philipon, and the establishment of *La Carica-ture* and afterward the *Charivari,* there began that curious struggle between half a dozen poor artists on one side and his majesty Louis Phillipe, his august family, and the numberless "placemen" and supporters of the monarchy on the other. ...Per-secutions, seizures, fines, made no impression of the dauntless little band, and week after week, with astounding ingenuity and variety of invention, the king of the French was held up to the laughter of Paris. The favorite device of Daumier was to play upon the resemblance the king's head bore to a pear, and soon the famous "pear" was chalked upon all the walls of the city. (1906, 245)

When Philipon was tried for inciting contempt against the king, at his trial he drew a pear, and then by adding lines here and there, reproduced a caricature of the king. "Is it my fault, gentlemen of the jury," he is reported to have said, "if his Majesty's face looks like a pear?" The book also contains several other similar cartoons: in one, "The Root of All Evil," Napoleon III is shown as a root, looking like a carrot with Napoleon III's features, and in a British cartoon that appeared in *Punch,* he is turned into a porcupine.

Political cartooning is alive and still vital. In America, we had the great Thomas Nast, who by himself is considered to have destroyed Boss Tweed (figure 10.2). Tweed is reported to have said "I don't care a straw for your newspaper articles. My constituents don't know how to read. But they can't help seeing them damned pictures," in discussing Nast's cartoons. We have continued his tradition with a number of brilliant political cartoonists such as Herblock, Bill Mauldin, Jeff MacNelly, Paul Conrad, Mike Peters, and Patrick Oliphant (an Australian by birth). Oliphant caricatures his "victims" brilliantly—some say viciously—and has created a number of biting cartoons that point to the failings of various political figures. He also uses a device taken from comic strips—a little character who makes humorous asides.

These political cartoons are often much stronger than written material, because it is much easier to ridicule someone, to make allusions about someone's transgressions and crimes, and to express content and loathing for someone visually by using caricatures than it is in prose. Cartoonists also tend to be immune from attack. In part this is because cartoonists are seen as humorists who deal with political and social con-

FIGURE 10.1

Philipon, "The Pears," *Le Charivari* January 17, 1831

FIGURE 10.2

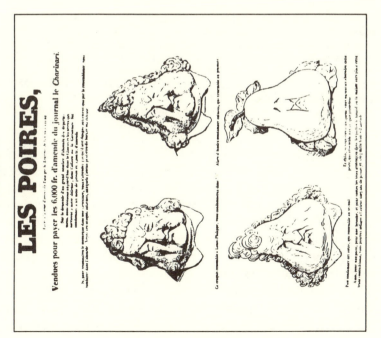

Thomas Nast, "A Group of Vultures Waiting for the Storm to 'Blow Over'—
'Let Us Prey,'" Harper's Weekly, September 23, 1871

cerns and, as humorists, are protected from lawsuits and politicians. The Supreme Court has defended the right of humorists to parody individuals and satirize their beliefs. It is political death in America to get into fights with humorists and comedians and to be seen as someone without a sense of humor.

Political cartoonists have a somewhat ambiguous status, since they can be seen as humorists who deal with serious political matters. By making us laugh about some political matter, do they diminish its significance and make us "not take it seriously"? Or, by calling attention to it, do they play an important role in shaping the political consciousness of their followers?

Those political cartoonists who are not syndicated and work for particular newspapers are, in principle, supposed to support the ideological beliefs of their owners. Therefore, some political cartoonists are really instruments of others—their editors—though we might assume that a cartoonist would not work for a paper whose editorial principles he or she didn't support. Edward Sorel, a great cartoonist, describes these "captive" cartoonists as "cartoon assassins."

As he writes in "The Limits on Drawing Power":

> Editorial pages have traditionally carried only one political cartoon and that practice has not changed. Furthermore, that single pictorial commentary is designed to express the opinion of the editorial board, not the artist who drew it. Likely as not, the cartoon is simply illustrating in graphic terms what the adjacent editorial is expressing in prose. Even in newspapers that do not dictate to their editorial cartoonist, the artist must always get clearance from the editor before the drawing is published....Editorial artists are, and always have been, little more than cartoon assassins with a list of permissible targets supplied by the editorial board. (1981, 30)

As a result, Sorel suggests, most cartoonists working for newspapers are second-rate talents. Thus, the first-rate talents, such as Jules Feiffer and David Levine, tend to be excluded from editorial pages and do not get their work carried in a large number of publications. What is needed, Sorel says, is for editorial cartoonists to be given the same kind of freedom that political columnists are given. Newspapers should not be allowed to maintain a double standard: one for political columnists and another for political cartoonists.

Garry Trudeau's *Doonesbury* is technically a comic strip, but it deals with social and political matters and some newspapers actually carry it on their editorial pages. Trudeau is a liberal who mounts savage attacks

on Republican politicians and policies, though he doesn't spare Democrats when he thinks they deserve attention. But the strip also deals with
social matters, fads, zany characters, and pokes fun at social trends with
as much relish as it does political figures. Trudeau's strips are so biting
that at certain times, when some newspapers consider a strip too strong
(or too much opposed to their ideological position), these newspapers
do not carry him for a day or so.

The situation described by Sorel may be changing somewhat as American society becomes more open and political commentary and humor
become more common. The Tonight Show (and other late-night television shows) often have a good deal of political humor in them and sav-
agely ridicule political figures for various transgressions.

Funny Optical Illusions

Optical illusions, by their very nature, are perceived as "funny" in
that they confuse us, often in amusing ways. The "Devil's Tuning Fork,"
for example, shows a tuning fork with three prongs, but our eyes get
confused when we try to attach the prongs to the base. Another optical
illusion presents us with the figure of a woman, but if looked at in a
different way, we see a face. The ambiguity of the drawing is the source
of amusement.

In some cases, artists use collections of objects to make a human face
and it is the ability of these objects to suggest something else that amuses
us. There's a political caricature of Teddy Roosevelt by L. C. Gregg
called "For President" that appeared in the *Atlanta Constitution*. It was

FIGURE 10.3

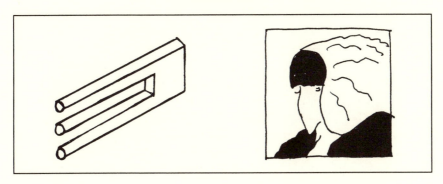

FIGURE 10.4

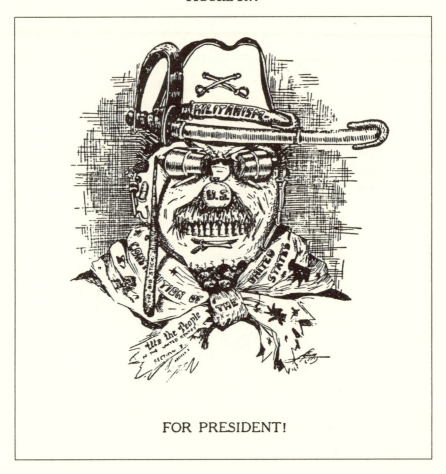

FOR PRESIDENT!

L.L. Gregg, "For President!" *Atlanta Constitution,* circa 1904.

created by assembling swords, cannons, and bullets to form his face, a technique used many centuries earlier by the Italian artist Arcimboldo. An earlier cartoon that used the same techniques appeared in 1828 and was drawn by David Claypoole Johnson. It is of Andrew Jackson, called "Richard III," and is made up of naked dead bodies, upposedly killed as the result of Jackson's violent temper.

Visual Riddles and Puns

These illusions might be described as visual puzzles or visual riddles that we have to solve. I have used the technique of making visual riddles, in conjunction with puns on the term *pawn* (figure 10.5) to make a number of amusing little drawings. I make a drawing of someone or something tied to the sound *pawn* and underneath it have some written material which helps the reader figure out who is being drawn or what the drawing is about. A number of these visual riddles follow.

In addition, I've drawn a number of visual puns, each of which involve the term *con* (figure 10.6). In each drawing, a con (as in convict) is drawn in a way that connects him to a word using "con," as in concave (in which a con is shown sitting in a cave) and content (in which a con is shown holding up a tent). A number of these drawings follow.

On Humorous Illustration

These "con" drawings suggest that there is often a relation between a concept (no pun intended) and a drawing. In fact, much humorous illustration is based on making some kind of a representation that alludes to an idea or concept, discussed in some textual material. The humor is created by making drawings using such techniques as caricature, exaggeration, allusion, parody, and facetiousness.

As an example of parody, there's a wonderful painting, "First Family," done in 1991 by Paul Bachem, that spoofs Jan Van Eyck's famous painting *Giovanni Arnolfini and His Bride* (figure 10.7) done in 1434. The Van Eyck shows a rich Italian and his bride, who is pregnant (a symbol of her willingness to bear children) and is full of other symbols that people at that time would have recognized. The Bachem parody is of George and Barbara Bush and replaces the medieval symbols with newspapers and photos that call attention to political matters. It is the caricatures of George and Barbara Bush and the intertextual allusions to Van Eyck that create the humor in the Bachem painting. Those who do not know the Van Eyck painting would still find the Bachem painting humorous, due to the caricatures and strange clothing the Bushes are wearing, but wouldn't get the full force of the humor.

Let me offer some examples from the drawings that I have done for *The Journal of Communication*. For more than a dozen years I drew

FIGURE 10.5

① Native American Pawn   ② Famous Explorer

③ A Religious Leader   ④ Where Pawns Live   ⑤ Political Club

⑥ Famous Gangster   ⑦ Frenchman Thinking   ⑧ Planes Pawns Fly

1. Pawnee 2. Ponce de Leon 3. Pontiff 4. Ponderosa Territory 5. Ripon Society 6. Al Capone 7. Pensees 8. Pontoon

FIGURE 10.6

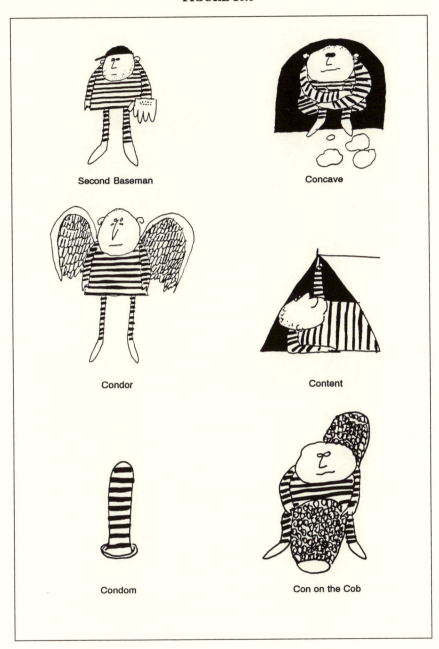

Second Baseman

Concave

Condor

Content

Condom

Con on the Cob

FIGURE 10.7

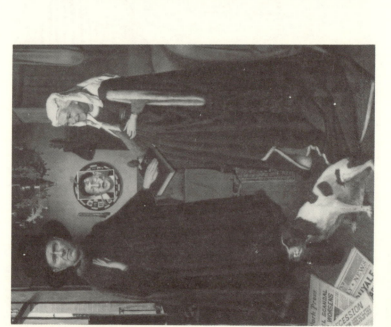

Jan Van Eyck, *Giovanni Arnolfini and His Bride*

Paul Bachem, *First Family*

FIGURE 10.8

Arthur Asa Berger, "The Secret Agent," *Journal of Communication,* 1974.

illustrations for this publication. The editors would send me photocopies of various articles and book reviews and I would make a number of drawings relating to some aspect of the articles or reviews—some topic that was mentioned or some concept that was dealt with.

The basic problem one faces when making humorous illustrations for textual material is finding something to draw that relates to the topics discussed in the article. In semiotic terms, the concept is a signified and the artist looks for visual signifiers. One essay I did an illustration for was about electronic banking. What I had to do was find some visual way of suggesting electronic banking that was also amusing. The drawing I came up with was a pig with an electric cord for its tail. I decided that a pig with a slot in its back (a piggy bank) suggested banking and that a cord with a plug suggested electric or electronic, so when you put the pig and the cord together you got electronic banking. This drawing has no written matter in it, though, as I've explained, many humorous illustrations do use text—either things that comic characters say or captions meant to provide an amusing commentary on things.

FIGURE 10.9

Electronic Banking

An illustration I did for a review of a book on advertising shows a man holding a sign saying "Advertising does not work." The humor in this case involves using advertising (the sign) to suggest, paradoxically, that advertising doesn't work. The drawing itself is not particularly amusing but the concept of using advertising to argue, ironically, that advertising is ineffective is entertaining, or so, at least, I thought (and so did the editor of the journal). Humorous illustrations are not meant to generate laughter but, perhaps, a faint smile of bemusement. They are used to call attention to certain aspects of an article and, on a more mundane level, to break up masses of gray text.

Conclusions

By using such techniques as caricature, exaggeration, allusion, and facetiousness comic strip artists, cartoonists, and illustrators can create powerful and extremely effective humorous texts. The artists can also use language—in most cartoons and in comic strips, wordplay and language usage often has a major role in generating the humor. We now find cartoons, comics, and other forms of visual humor playing increasingly important roles in our politics and entertainments of all kinds, from films to greeting cards. Our political cartoonists are analogous to the fools of earlier days, except that we tend to take our cartoonists more seriously. We get a double payoff. We are amused at the humor and we also are forced to consider something a politician has done or give thought to some political issue that is of importance.

Visual phenomena, from optical illusions to caricatures, play an important role in humor, and much of the humor that we experience from day to day has a visual dimension to it. I'm talking here about cartoons and comic strips, which we read in the daily newspapers, and also about the way actors and actresses use extreme facial expressions and body language to generate laughter in the situation comedies we watch on television and in the humorous films we see. There are, in addition, visual puns and sight gags. So a look often leads to a laugh.

References

Berger, Arthur Asa. *The Comic-Stripped American*. New York: Walker & Co, 1974.

———. *Li'l Abner: A Study in American Satire*. Jackson: University Press of Mississippi, 1994 (originally published by Twayne in 1970).

Harris, Joel Chandler, et al., eds. *The World's Wit and Humor,* vol. XI. New York: The Review of Reviews, 1906.

Inge, M. Thomas. *Comics as Culture*. Jackson: University Press of Mississippi, 1990.

Maurice, Arthur Bartlett. *The World's Wit and Humor: French*. New York: The Review of Reviews Company, 1906.

Sorel, Edward. "The Limits on Drawing Power." *Washington Journalism Review* (October 1981).

*...In the beginning, when the world was
young there were a great many thoughts but
no such thing as a truth. Man made the
truths himself and each truth was a compos-
ite of a great many vague thoughts. All about
in the world were the truths and they were
beautiful.... And then the people came
along. Each as he appeared snatched up one
of the truths and some who were quite strong
snatched up a dozen of them. It was the
truths that made the people grotesques...
the moment one of the people took one of the
truths to himself, called it his truth, and tried
to live his life by it, he became a grotesque
and the truth he embraced became a
falsehood.*

—Sherwood Anderson
Winesburg, Ohio

11

After the Laughter: A Concluding Note

I hope that the case studies I have offered provided some interesting and useful insights about the way people in various disciplines and adherents of various methodologies make sense of humor. As we have seen, humor is a very slippery subject. It is so pervasive, so incredibly complicated, has so many forms and modes of expression, and does so many things for so many people that it is hard to get a grip on it, to contain it.

The Difficulties Involved in Dealing with Humor

Humor plays a big role in our conversations where it is sometimes used to control people and in other cases used to resist control and domination by others. Humor is involved in our relationships and studies have shown that men and women look for a sense of humor in their partners. Humor plays a big role in the mass media, where situation comedies are one of the most significant broadcast genres and comedies are a major genre in our films. We find humor in the elite arts as well—in the plays, novels, and stories of our greatest writers from the comedies of the earliest Greek writers to playwrights and novelists in the present day. In his book on Rabelais, M. M. Bakhtin has written about the role of humor in the Middle Ages and the spirit of what he called "carnivalization" that characterized this period. Humor, I would suggest, brings us a momentary experience of this spirit of carnivalization Bakhtin wrote about.

We find humor so variegated and multiform that it has eluded attempts by those who study it to deal with it, especially those who try to determine what humor is and why we find things humorous. Nevertheless, there are some things that we can say about humor that help illuminate it. In this discussion, as in the book, I will assume that there is a strong relationship between humor, mirth, laughter, a feeling of joyfulness and elation, and related matters—even though we know that in some cases laughter is not connected with humor but with release from stress or with certain neurological and psychological afflictions.

Laughter Demolishes Fear and Piety

Bakhtin discusses this role humor plays in a passage in his book *The Dialogic Imagination* (1981, 23):

> It is precisely laughter that destroys the epic, and in general destroys any hierarchical (distancing and valorized) distance. At a distanced image a subject cannot be comical; to be made comical, it must be brought close. Everything that makes us laugh is close at hand, all comical creativity works in a zone of maximal proximity.

Fear and piety require an element of solemnity and high seriousness and a sense of distance so that spectacle can sway people in a crowd. But laughter, Bakhtin tells us, destroys that distancing necessary for spectacle and makes things close and familiar. Humor makes it possible for people to come close to objects, to see things as they really are, and penetrate the fog of spectacle and drama that are used by demagogues to delude people and sway their opinions.

Laughter, then, has played a role in history and in the Middle Ages, when there was a culture that honored laughter; humor and its ally, what Bakhtin described as popular speech, prevented a number of institutional excesses (or helped moderate things) and played an important role in people's everyday lives.

In the contemporary world, wherever there is free speech (and even in some places where there is not free speech) humor often exists as a critique of political arrangements and the status quo (think of the wonderful jokes about Russia and the Eastern European satellites that existed before the fall of communism), and our comedians have, among other things, taken on the role of making politicians familiar and ridiculing them. Therefore, humor is intimately connected with political freedom. At the same time humor is also responsible, it seems, for the sense of personal and psychological liberation that people feel when they have had a good laugh.

Often, of course, our laughter is at someone else's expense. Thus, ethnic humor provides us with a good laugh and a sense of elation, but at the expense of the groups being ridiculed. For example, consider this classic Polish joke—one from a cycle of Polish jokes that were popular in America in recent years:

A Polish biology professor is conducting research on the nervous system of frogs. He takes a frog out of his tank, puts it on a table, and says "jump!" The frog jumps. He then takes a scalpel and cuts off one of the frog's front legs. The professor then says "jump!" and the frog jumps. The professor cuts off the other front leg of the frog and then says "jump!" The frog balances on his back legs and manages a decent jump. Then the professor cuts off one of the hind legs of the frog. The professor then says "jump!" The frog, bleeding profusely, manages a feeble hop. Finally, the professor cuts off the remaining leg of the frog and says "jump!" The frog doesn't do anything. The professor repeats himself, in a louder voice. "JUMP!" The frog does nothing. "I said jump," says the professor one last time. The frog does nothing. At this point the professor takes out his notebook and carefully notes, "when all limbs are amputated, it is observed that the frog becomes deaf."

This joke deals with the common stereotype of Poles as stupid. It is a bit unusual in that it is a long, rather elaborate joke—that is, a comic narrative, meant to amuse, with a punch line. Most of the time, the Polish jokes were not actually jokes but took the form of riddles, such as the ones that follow:

What has an IQ of 450?
Poland.

How do you break a Pole's finger?
Punch him in the nose.

How was the guy who won ten million dollars in the Polish lottery paid?
He gets ten dollars a year for a million years.

As a result of the assertiveness of various ethnic, racial, and sexual groups, these jokes, and ethnic jokes in general, are no longer considered acceptable or proper, but the joking tendency in people, found in our folklore and passed on by everything from word of mouth to telephone to fax and e-mail, refuses to be contained and only waits for other subjects to present themselves—as the material to come shows.

Humor Conveys Information

There is nonsense humor, in which characters babble meaningless sounds and phrases and sentences that don't make sense, which tells us relatively little (though we can infer things about the person making the nonsense humor). But jokes, as I pointed out in my chapter on communication theory, because they contain an element of surprise in their punch lines, do convey a considerable amount of information—according to communication theorists such as Claude Shannon. That is because unpredictability in messages is seen as being connected to the amount of information being given. If a person tells you something you already know, then, for all practical purposes, there's been no information passed on to you.

Thus, jokes qualify as being information rich, we might say, because we don't know what the punch line is going to be. But all kinds of humor convey information—both about the psyche and state of mind of the person creating the humor (or telling a joke, for example) and about the individuals, groups, societies, and cultures that are the subjects of the jokes or the humor. Consider the following joke:

> *Did you hear about the spelling bee between former Vice-President Dan Quayle and Senator Bob Packwood? Guess who won? Dan Quayle! Senator Packwood thought "harass" was two words.*

This joke is full of allusions to American political life. It alludes to the spelling bee at which Quayle misspelled "potato" (putting an extra "e" on it, as in "potatoe") and to Senator Packwood's notorious sexual behavior. In the joke, he thought "harass" was spelled "her ass." Both men are made, so to speak, "ignorant" in the joke.

The joke is not particularly funny, but it is intimately connected with American political life during the past couple of years. A person from a different country who knows nothing about either Quayle or Packwood would find the joke confusing, since it relies so heavily, as many political jokes do, on knowing the characters involved.

Let me offer one more political joke. This one deals with former president Ronald Reagan:

> *At a doctors convention in Switzerland, some doctors from different countries are talking in a tavern after the lectures for the day have concluded. An Israeli doctors says, "Medicine in Israel is so advanced that we can take a kidney out of one person and put it in another person and have him looking for work in four weeks." A German physician says "That's nothing! In Germany we can take a lung out of one person and put it in another person and have him looking for work in two weeks." Not wanting to be outdone, an American doctor says, "That's nothing! We can take an asshole out of Hollywood, put him in the White House, and have half the country looking for work the next day!"*

This joke alludes to the supposed impact of Reagan and his policies on the American economy. It is a joke that Democrats would find funny but that many Republicans might not consider terribly amusing. The joke uses a standard technique: theme and variation, dealing with medicine in Israel, Germany, and the United States. It also uses insult, calling Reagan an "asshole."

Let us turn now to the highly publicized matter of Michael Jackson's alleged pedophilia, which has generated a number of humorous riddles:

> *What do Michael Jackson and Pepsi-Cola have in common?*
> *They both come in small cans!*

> *What do Michael Jackson and K-Mart have in common?*
> *They both have boys pants half off!*

Another version of this latter riddle is:

> *What do Michael Jackson and K-Mart have in common?*
> *Boys underwear, half off!*

These riddles are tied to a significant and deeply troubling matter currently being discussed in American culture and society, the way we treat children (and, in particular, the matter of pedophilia), and to Jackson's eccentric personality.

What we can say here is that not only do jokes and riddles (and other forms of humor) deal with social and political matters of consequence (through allusions and other techniques), but also that they are good indicators of what is of interest to people at a given point in time and are often connected to news events, sometimes ones that are trivial and other times of major consequence.

Using the Techniques of Humor

In my chapter on rhetoric I have isolated and listed, in alphabetic order, the forty-five techniques that, I suggest, humorists use, in various combinations and permutations, to generate humor and laughter. Traditionally, rhetoric was developed as a means of persuading people, but I have modified this original understanding of rhetoric and, with my techniques, dealt with how we "persuade" people to find something humorous.

In essence I have refocused rhetorical theory in the direction of understanding the mechanisms that humorists use. Humorists, whether they be writers or comedians, I would suggest, are not generally aware of their use of these techniques. They write intuitively, but the methods they use are the ones I've listed (and, in some cases, are reversals of a given technique, such as turning "insult" on its head and using "victim" humor).

The techniques that a given humorist favors offer us, I would suggest, a sense of his or her comedic "style." It is possible, for example, to analyze the methods Shakespeare used in his early comedies and compare them with the techniques he used in his later ones, to see whether he changed his basic techniques. If so, we can pinpoint, with much greater accuracy, how he evolved as a writer of comedies. We can do the same thing with comic strip artists, stand-up comedians, cartoonists, novelists, and other kinds of humorists.

We can also use the techniques to study folklore, compare graffiti bathrooms in various ways (men's bathrooms and women's bathrooms, bathrooms in working-class places and upper-class places), and find many other ways of using the techniques to gain more precision in the way we deal with humor.

These techniques need some kind of a "play" frame to be seen as generating humor. Insult, by itself, is highly aggressive and not funny. In a "play" frame, in which we know we aren't to take the insults seriously, they take on a different meaning. Comedians, by definition, are supposed to be funny and so generate a "play" element in their routines. There is, in the monologues of comedians, generally a lot of aggression and insulting, but we have learned that comedians are "not to be taken seriously" so this kind of behavior is seen as acceptable. The same applies to jokes, which we all know are meant to stir laughter and amusement, even though they often insult and degrade all kinds of people : politicians, women, gays, dogs, psychiatrists, artists, the clergy, ethnic groups, racial groups, religious groups, groups with particular sexual orientations, people who have problems screwing in light bulbs, elephants, you name it.

Playwrights use funny names, eccentric characters, bizarre behavior, and other such things to establish a "play" frame. We have to recognize this "play" frame, otherwise we might take insults, exaggeration, absurdity, and the other techniques the wrong way. In some cases, we have a combination of seriousness and "play" and it becomes difficult to determine what is going on and how one should interpret a given bit of dialogue or behavior, but we've all had so much experience with humor that we generally understand what to make of dialogue. That is why irony is so problematic. The addressee must somehow recognize—either by the tone of voice or the context of the statement—that one is being ironic. Often this does not happen and an ironic statement is misunderstood. This leads to my next topic, the problem of how people make sense of humor—a constant thread in this book.

The Problem of Audiences

I have dealt with the problem of how individuals "read" (decode, make sense of) texts of all kinds in my discussion of reader-response theory. This theory anatomizes audiences into discrete individuals, each of whom makes sense of a text in his or her own way. The mass media can bring television shows or films to millions of people, but, according to the reader-response theorists (or reception theorists), everyone interprets a text in his or her own way. If that is so, why do people in an audience seeing a film tend to laugh at the same time?

Aaron Wildavsky's work on political culture suggests that the radical decomposing of audiences that reader-response theory implies may not be correct. What Wildavsky (and his colleagues who have worked with him in various books) found was that there are four political cultures in democratic societies and that individuals interpreted things (and made decisions) on the basis of their identification with one of these four groups: hierarchists or elitists, individualists, egalitarians, and fatalists. (The chapter on humor and politics in this book represents a collaboration with Wildavsky, as a matter of fact. I used his theory and he supplied some of the jokes and made some suggestions, but he died before he was able to do much more than that.)

Wildavsky's theory enables us to negotiate our way between the Scylla of atomic individualism, with each person making sense of the world his or her way, and the Charybdis of mass society theories, with everyone marching in lock step and reacting to texts more or less the same way. Previous political theories, such as Marxism, for example, had divided the world into two groups: an elite that ran everything and controlled everyone; and a mass of people that opposed this group, but lacked self-knowledge and cohesion. Other political theorists created different bipolar oppositions.

For Wildavsky, there were four dominant political cultures, not two, and membership in a political culture allowed individuals with little information (about the political world, for example) to make choices about all kinds of things—on the basis of whether the values and beliefs of one's political culture would be strengthened or weakened and the goals furthered if someone were elected and some proposal passed into law.

In the same light, people in each political culture would, more or less, find certain jokes and other texts and works humorous and react negatively to jokes and texts not congruent with their beliefs and values. It is assumed that people want to have their beliefs and values reinforced and want to avoid dissonance, which is generated when their beliefs and values are attacked. In some cases, in which it is difficult to determine which group is being attacked, it was suggested that jokes and other humor could be seen as high or low grid, for example.

Let me offer a typical hierarchist or elitist joke—one that ridicules elements "below" those at the top. This joke is a Russian joke that makes fun of a group of people, the Chukchi people, who play the same role in Russian jokes that Poles play in American jokes and the Irish play in English jokes.

> *A Chukchi man goes to a store to buy a television set. The clerk tells him that color sets are available. "Fine," says the Chukchi, "I'll have a yellow one."*

The basic techniques in this joke are stereotyping (Chukchi are stupid) and misunderstanding (when the clerk mentions color sets, the Chukchi thinks the clerk is talking about the color of the sets, not that they broadcast in color).

Consider, now, an egalitarian joke—one that pokes fun at powerful and rich business and political figures:

> *President Reagan and Nancy go to a restaurant for lunch. The waiter asks Nancy Reagan for her order first. "I'll have the grilled salmon and a cup of coffee," she says. "What about the vegetable?" asks the waiter. "He'll have the same thing," Nancy replies.*

Reagan's age and reputation for falling asleep at Cabinet meetings and taking naps all the time was the source of the humor here—using the techniques of allusion and misunderstanding. When the waiter asked Nancy about the vegetable, he meant a vegetable to go with her salmon, but Nancy misunderstood the question and took it as a reference to Reagan. I think it is pretty easy to describe this joke as essentially an egalitarian one. This same joke, incidentally, is also told about Supreme

Court Justice Sandra Day O'Connor and certain elderly members of the Supreme Court.

The joke depends on the listener knowing about Reagan, his age, and his work and sleep habits. Allusion is a technique that involves a figure/ground relationship. The joke makes Reagan a figure who becomes comic against the ground or background of his age and his work habits. Reagan has, it turns out, a wonderful sense of humor and used humor effectively all during his political career: to disarm opponents, to reassure the country (when he was shot), and to make himself popular with the general public. This amiability and sense of humor led to him being described as a "charming demagogue."

Ignorance and Discrepant Awareness

One of the themes that pervades this book, and many scholarly studies of humor, involves the matter of how people interpret humor, a topic I have discussed in some detail. Another is the matter of ignorance and discrepant awareness. This latter term refers to knowledge that members of an audience have (and, in some cases, some characters in a play have) that other characters do not have. If there is discrepant awareness, it means that some character, in a joke or play or whatever, is unaware of something, is ignorant, and others know what is going on.

Comedy frequently involves characters who lack self-knowledge, who are unaware of what they are really like, of what people think of them, of the way they are driven by passions, of the extent to which they are comic monomaniacs or grotesques or fools. In some cases, characters lack information about what is happening. They are, in a sense, rendered ignorant or made stupid—of their own situation, if nothing else. Ethnic humor, as I pointed out, often involves creating stupid groups— Polish people (in America), Irish people (in England), and so on.

But this discrepant awareness permeates our humor; it is not limited to plays, by any means. Thus, when we listen to a joke we are, in a sense, rendered ignorant, for we don't know how the joke will proceed and how it will all turn out. It is the punch line that provides us with the information we need and turns us from being "ignorant" to being knowledgeable. Members of the audience of a joke teller experience a collective kind of discrepant awareness, and thus, in a sense, are made comic themselves.

There is something ironic about this: we laugh at the characters in the joke who are ignorant and foolish, but that's the way we were before we heard the punch line. And irony itself is based to a great extent on discrepant awareness, since someone who says something ironic, which is not recognized as ironic, is rendering his or his listeners ignorant. There is a discrepant awareness relative to the speaker and the listener or listeners.

In the case of dramatic irony, in plays, for example, it is the character who says something (that turns out to be ironic) who suffers from discrepant awareness. Other characters in the play may recognize the ironic nature of the statement, but the character who says something that turns out to be ironic does not—and, in many cases, neither do members of the audience.

One of the things that appeals to us in comedies is the way we finally get to find out what is really happening and are made knowledgeable. Comedies are much more complicated than tragedies—which generally have a direct, rather linear nature. Comedies are messes, full of complications and complexities that have to be cleared up or resolved in logically and emotionally satisfying ways. The resolutions in comedies often involve ironic twists, as is the case in *Volpone* in which a charlatan who has outwitted others finally outwits himself.

Dealing with Complexity

It is the complexity of humor that poses problems for those scholars who work with it. In the first issue of *Humor: International Journal of Humor Research,* Mahadev Apte writes about the difficulties he found when he started studying humor. As he writes in his essay "Disciplinary Boundaries in Humorology: An Anthropologist's Rumination" (1988, 8).

> Ever since I began research on humor I have been struck by the elusive nature of the phenomenon and by the diverse disciplinary backgrounds and orientations of scholars interested in it. While diversity of theoretical orientation and individualistic concerns are a very common occurrence in anthropology, which, according to some of its practitioners, is so amorphous as not to be a discipline at all, I was not prepared for the diversity and variation I found in the literature on humor. This meant gaining familiarity with the major issues involved in humor research through reading vast amounts of material, learning technical terms and concepts employed by scholars in disciplines ranging from literary criticism to ethology, and finally, trying to discern and understand the methodologies employed for investigating certain aspects of humor.

Apte goes on to mention that studying humor has been "a stepchild of academe," which previously had little status in university circles. But in the past decade and a half, he notes, there's been an explosion of interest in humor in university circles and elsewhere. (He suggests the term *humorology* for the study of humor, a term I am personally uncomfortable with and find rather awkward.) Humor has always been an important part of the mass media, of course, but now there is a humor channel and there was the explosive growth of comedy clubs all through America during the 1980s.

Apte points out one of the most difficult aspects of humor research. He writes (1988, 11):

> A major problem is that most scholars who have been engaged in humor research have approached it from their own disciplinary orientation; thus they have focused on different aspects of the phenomenon. This has resulted in humor receiving different identities. That the debate about what humor is is not new is illustrated by the fact that in a major publication in 1972 at the start of the current resurgence of humor research, the editors declined to define the concept (Goldstein and McGhee 1972:xxi). In another major publication more recently the same scholars state that "there is still no agreement on how humor should be defined" (McGhee and Goldstein 1983:vi), despite their view that research on humor has accelerated tremendously in the last 15 years and that a thorough bibiography on humor and laughter would contain several thousand items.

In the years since 1983, of course, there have been countless other articles and books on the subject. It still remains problematic and difficult, and one that lends itself best, due to the nature of its extreme complexity, I have argued, to a multidisciplinary approach. And that is what I have offered in this book. But how one best integrates the different approaches of "humorologists" who come from so many different approaches, disciplines, and perspectives, remains a puzzle.

They're All Right

I cannot end this book on the way people from different disciplines and adherents of various methodologies approach humor without one last bit of comic relief—an old Jewish story that is, I suggest, relevant to our concerns.

> *A woman comes to a rabbi in a highly distressed state. She askes if the rabbi would see her. He agrees. She then starts complaining to him about her husband. She recites a long litany of terrible things her husband has done. From time to time, as*

she tells her story, the rabbi nods his head and says "You're right, you're right."
After complaining about her husband, the woman is greatly relieved. She thanks
the rabbi and leaves. An hour later, a man, wildly agitated, comes to see the rabbi
and begs to see him. The rabbi agrees. It is the husband of the woman who had
previously seen the rabbi. The man tells his side of the story and offers a long tale
of his wife's failings, disputing everything that she had said about him. As he talks,
the rabbi nods, from time to time, and says "You're right, you're right." When the
man finishes, he too is relieved and in a much calmer mood, leaves. The rabbi's
wife, it turns out, had been in the room listening to both the man and the woman.
"How can you agree with the wife and then also agree with the husband, when they
both told contradictory stories about each other? It doesn't make sense." "You're
right," said the rabbi... "you're absolutely right."

Conclusions

Each perspective on humor dealt with in this book has interesting
things to say and insights to offer, but none of them is "the whole truth"
about humor. This may be, of course, because there is no "whole truth"
to humor, there is no way to deal with it, in part because it takes so many
forms and is so complicated. But in seeing it from a number of different
perspectives, in offering a number of case histories showing how individuals from a variety disciplinary perspectives make sense of it, or, to
be more precise, some aspect of it, I would hope that our appreciation
and understanding of humor has been enhanced.

References

Apte, Mahadev L. "Disciplinary Boundaries in Humorology: An Anthropologist's
    Ruminations." *Humor: International Journal of Humor Research*, vol. 1 (1988).
Bakhtin, M. M. *The Dialogic Imagination*, edited by M. Holquist and translated by
    Caryl Emerson and Michael Holquist. Austin: University of Texas Press, 1981.
Berger, Arthur Asa. *An Anatomy of Humor*. New Brunswick, NJ: Transaction Publish-
    ers, 1993.

Bibliography

Abrams, M. H. *A Glossary of Literary Terms*. New York: Holt, Rinehart & Winston, 1961.

Adams, J. *Ethnic Humor*. New York: Manor Books, 1975.

Allen, S. *Funny Man*. New York: Simon & Shuster, 1956.

Allen, Woody. *Getting Even*. New York: Vantage, 1978.

———. *Side Effects*. New York: Ballantine, 1981.

Alter, Robert. *Rogue's Progress*. Cambridge, MA: Harvard University Press, 1964.

Apte, M. L. *Humor and Laughter: An Anthropological Approach*. Ithaca, NY: Cornell University Press, 1985.

———. "Disciplinary Boundaries in Humorology: An Anthropologist's Ruminations." *Humor,* vol. 1, no. 1 (1988).

Anderson, Sherwood. *Winesburg, Ohio*. New York: Signet Books, 1956.

Ashbee, C. R. *Caricature*. London: Chapman & Hall, Ltd., 1928.

Attardo, Salvatore, and Jean-Charles Chabanne. "Jokes as a Text Type." *Humor,* vol. 5, nos. 1/2 (1992).

Ausubel, Nathan. *A Treasury of Jewish Humor*. New York: Doubleday, 1951.

———. *A Treasury of Jewish Folklore*. New York: Crown Publishers, 1978.

Bakhtin, Mikhail. *The Dialogic Imagination,* edited by Michael Holquist and translated by Caryl Emerson and Michael Holquist. Austin: University of Texas Press, 1981.

———. *Rabelais and His World*. Bloomington: Indiana University Press, 1984.

Becker, Stephen. *Comic Art in America*. New York: Simon & Schuster, 1959.

Bennett, D. J. "The Psychological Meaning of Anti-Negro Jokes." *Fact* (1964).

Berger, Arthur Asa. *Li'l Abner: A Study in American Satire*. New York: Twayne Publishers, 1970. (Being reprinted by University Press of Mississippi, 1994).

———. "Was Krazy's Creator a Black Cat?" *San Francisco Examiner* (*This World Magazine*), 22 August 1971.

———. *The Comic-Stripped American*. New York: Walker & Co., 1973.

———. "The Secret Agent." *Journal of Communication* (1974).

———. *The TV-Guided American*. New York: Walker & Co., 1975.

———. "Huck Finn as an Existential Hero." *Mark Twain Journal* (Summer, 1976).

———. "Anatomy of the Joke." *Journal of Communication,* vol. 26, no. 3 (1976).

———, ed. "Humor, The Psyche and Society." *American Behavioral Scientist,* vol. 30, no. 3 (January/February 1987).

———. "Comics and Popular Culture." *The World & I,* vol. 5, no. 7 (1990).

Bergler, Edmund. *Laughter and the Sense of Humor*. New York: Intercontinental Medical Book Co., 1956.

Bettelheim, Bruno. *The Uses of Enchantment: The Meaning and Importance of Fairy Tales*. New York: Knopf, 1976.

Blair, Walter. *Native American Humor*. San Francisco: Chandler Publishing Co., 1960.

Boatright, Moady. *Folk Laughter on the American Frontier.* New York: Collier Books, 1961.

Boskin, J. *Humor and Social Change in Twentieth Century America.* Boston: The Public Library of the City of Boston, 1979.

Botkin, B. A. *A Treasury of American Folklore.* New York: Crown Publishers, 1944.

Brewer, John, and Albert Hunter. *Multimethod Research: A Synthesis of Styles.* Newbury Park, CA: Sage Publications, 1989.

Brody, M. "The Wonderful World of Disney—It's Psychological Appeal." Unpublished manuscript, 1975.

Burke, Kenneth. *Terms for Order,* edited by Stanley Edgar Hyman. Bloomington: Indiana University Press, 1964.

Cameron, William Bruce. *Informal Sociology.* New York: Random House, 1963.

Cantril, Hadley, and Gordon W. Allport. *The Psychology of Radio.* New York: Peter Smith, 1941.

Capp, Al. *The Life and Times of the Shmoo.* New York: Simon & Schuster, 1948.

Chapman, Tony, and Hugh Foot, eds. *Humor and Laughter: Theory, Research and Applications.* London: John Wiley & Sons, 1976.

Charney, Maurice. *Comedy High & Low.* New York: Oxford University Press, 1978.

Cousins, Norman. *Anatomy of an Illness.* New York: W.W. Norton & Co., 1979.

Davies, Christie. "An Explanation of Jewish Jokes about Jewish Women." *Humor* vol. 3, no.4 (1990).

———. *Ethnic Humor Around the World.* Bloomington: Indiana University Press, 1990.

Douglas, Mary. *Implicit Meanings: Essays in Anthropology.* London: Routledge & Kegan Paul, 1975.

———. *In the Active Voice.* London: Routledge & Kegan Paul, 1982.

Duncan, H.D. *Language & Literature in Society.* Chicago: University of Chicago Press, 1953.

Dundes, Alan. *Cracking Jokes: Studies of Sick Humor Cycles and Stereotypes.* Berkeley, CA: Ten Speed Press, 1987.

Dundes, Alan, and Roger Abrahams. "On Elephantasy and Elephanticide." *The Psychoanalytic Review,* vol. 56, no. 2 (1969).

Eco, Umberto. *The Role of the Reader: Explorations in the Semiotics of Texts.* Bloomington: Indiana University Press, 1984.

Ehrenberg, Victor. *The People of Aristophanes.* New York: Schocken Books, 1962.

Elliot, Bob, and Ray Goulding. *From Approximately Coast to Coast It's the Bob and Ray Show.* New York: Penguin Books, 1985.

Esar, Evan. *The Humor of Humor.* New York: Bramhill House, 1952.

———. *The Comic Encyclopedia.* Garden City, NY: Doubleday, 1978.

Feinberg, Leonard. *The Satirist: His Temperament, Motivation and Influence.* Ames: Iowa State University Press, 1963.

Felheim, Marvin, ed. *Comedy: Plays, Theory and Criticism.* New York: Harcourt, Brace & World, Inc., 1962.

Freud, Sigmund. *Jokes and Their Relation to the Unconscious.* New York: W.W. Norton & Co., 1963.

———. "Character and Anal Eroticism." In *Sigmund Freud: Character and Culture,* edited by Philip Rieff. New York: Collier Books, 1963.

Fry, William. *Sweet Madness: A Study of Humor.* Palo Alto, CA: Pacific Books, 1963.

———. "Using Humor to Save Lives." Address to the American Orthopsychiatry Association, Washington, D.C. (1979).

Fry, William, and Melanie Allen. *Make 'Em Laugh: Life Studies of Comedy Writers*. Palo Alto, CA: Science & Behavior Books, 1975.

Fry, William, and Waleed A. Salameh, eds. *Handbook of Humor and Psychotherapy*. Sarasota, FL: Professional Resource Exchange, 1986.

Frye, Northrop. *Anatomy of Criticism*. Princeton, NJ: Princeton University Press, 1957.

Graña, Cesar. *Modernity and Its Discontents*. New York: Harper, 1976.

Grotjahn, Martin. *Beyond Laughter: Humor and the Subconscious*. New York: McGraw Hill, 1966.

Gruner, Charles. *Understanding Laughter: The Workings of Wit and Humor*. Chicago: Nelson-Hall, 1978.

Harris, Joel Chandler, et al., eds. *The World's Wit and Humor*, vol. XI. New York: The Review of Reviews, 1906.

Harrison, Randall. *The Cartoon: Communication to the Quick*. Beverley Hills, CA: Sage Publications, 1981.

Hebdidge, D. *Subculture: The Meaning of Style*. London: Methuen, 1979.

Helitzer, Melvin. *Comedy Writing Secrets*. Cincinnati: Writer's Digest Books, 1987.

Highet, Gilbert. *The Anatomy of Satire*. Princeton, NJ: Princeton University Press, 1962.

Hinsie, Leland E., and Robert Jean Campbell. *Psychiatric Dictionary* (fourth edition). New York: Oxford University Press, 1970.

Hobbes, Thomas. *Leviathan*. Oxford: Basic Blackwell, 1957.

Hoffman, D. G. *Form and Fable in American Fiction*. New York: Oxford University Press, 1961.

Hoffman, Werner. *Caricature from Leonardo to Picasso*. London: John Calder, 1957.

Horowitz, Irving Louis. *The Decomposition of Sociology*. New York: Oxford University Press, 1993.

Howe, Irving, and Eliezer Greenberg, eds. *A Treasury of Yiddish Stories*. New York: Schocken, 1974.

Hyers, Conrad. *Zen and the Comic Spirit*. Philadelphia: Westminster, 1974.

Inge, M. Thomas. *Comics as Culture*. Jackson: University Press of Mississippi, 1990.

Kayser, Wolfgang. *The Grotesque: In Art and Literature*. Bloomington: Indiana University Press, 1963.

Klapp, Orrin E. *Heroes, Villains and Fools: The Changing American Character*. Englewood Cliffs, NJ: Prentice-Hall, 1962.

Klein, Allen. *The Healing Power of Humor*. Los Angeles: Jeremy P. Tarcher, 1989.

Koestler, Arthur. *Insight and Outlook*. New York: Macmillan, 1949.

Kris, Ernst. *Psychoanalytic Explorations in Art*. New York: International University Press, 1952.

Kubie, Lawrence. "The Destructive Potential of Humor in Psychotherapy." In *A Celebration of Laughter*, edited by Werner Mendel. Los Angeles: Mara Books, 1970.

Legman, Gershon. *Rationale of the Dirty Joke*. New York: Grove Press, 1968.

Levin, Harry. *Playboys and Killjoys: An Essay on the Theory & Practices of Comedy*. New York: Oxford University Press, 1987.

Levine, Jacob, ed. *Motivation in Humor*. New York: Atherton Press, 1969.

Lodge, David. *Modern Criticism and Theory: A Reader*. New York: Longman, 1988.

Lynn, Kenneth. *Mark Twain and Southwestern Humor*. Boston: Atlantic Little-Brown, 1959.

McGhee, Paul E. *Humor: Origins and Development*. San Francisco, CA: W.H.Freeman & Co., 1979.

McGhee, Paul E., and Jeffrey H. Goldstein. *The Handbook of Humor Research*. New York: Springer-Verlag, 1983.

McKeon, Richard, ed. *The Basic Works of Aristotle*. New York: Random House, 1941.

Medhurst, Martin J., and Thomas W. Benson, eds. *Rhetorical Dimensions of Media: A Critical Casebook*. Dubuque, IA: Kendall/Hunt, 1984.

Mendel, Werner, ed. *A Celebration of Laughter*. Los Angeles: Mara Books, 1970.

Mindess, Harvey. *Laughter & Liberation*. Los Angeles: Nash Publishing, 1971.

———. "The Panorama of Humor and the Meaning of Life." In *American Behavioral Scientist*, vol. 30, no.3 (January/February 1987).

Monroe, D. H. *Argument of Laughter*. Melbourne: Melbourne University Press, 1951.

Morreall, J. *Taking Laughter Seriously*. Albany: State University of New York Press, 1983.

———. *The Philosophy of Laughter and Humor*. Albany: State University of New York Press, 1987.

Peter, Laurence J., and Bill Dana. *The Laughter Prescription*. New York: Ballantine, 1982.

Piddington, Ralph. *The Psychology of Laughter*. New York: Gamut Press, 1963.

Pierce, John, and A. Michael Noll. *Signals: The Science of Telecommunications*. New York: Scientific American Library, 1990.

Plessner, Helmuth. *Laughter and Crying*. Evanston, IL: Northwestern University Press, 1970.

Powell, Chris, and George E. C. Paton., eds. *Humour in Society: Resistance and Control*. New York: St. Martin's Press, 1988.

Primeau, Ronald. *The Rhetoric of Television*. New York: Longman, 1979.

Propp, Vladimir. *Morphology of the Folktale*. Austin: University of Texas Press, 1979.

Raskin, V. *Semantic Mechanism of Humor*. Dordecht: D. Reidel, 1985.

Rosenheim, E. W. *Swift and the Satirist's Art*. Chicago: University of Chicago Press, 1963.

Rosten, Leo. *The Joys of Yiddish*. Harmondsworth, England: Penguin, 1971.

Rourke, Constance. *American Humor: A Study of National Character*. New York: Doubleday Anchor Books, 1931.

Saussure, Ferdinand de. *Course in General Linguistics*. New York: McGraw-Hill, 1966.

Schickel, Richard. *The Disney Version*. New York: Avon Books, 1969.

Sebeok, Thomas A. *Sight, Sound and Sense*. Bloomington: Indiana University Press, 1978.

Sorel, Edward. "The Limits on Drawing Power." *Washington Journalism Review* (October 1981).

Sypher, Wylie, ed. *Comedy*. New York: Doubleday Anchor Books, 1956.

Thompson, Michael, Richard Ellis, and Aaron Wildavsky. *Cultural Theory*. Boulder, CO: Westview Press, 1990.

Twain, Mark. *Huckleberry Finn*. New York: Washington Square Press, 1960.

Wilson, Christopher P. *Jokes: Form, Content, Use and Function*. London: Academic Press, 1979.

Wolfenstein, Martha. *Children's Humor: A Psychological Analysis*. Bloomington: Indiana University Press, 1964.

Yates, Norris. *The American Humorist: Conscience of the Twentieth Century*. Ames: Iowa State University Press, 1964.

Vernon, Enid, ed. *Humor in America: An Anthology*. New York: Harcourt Brace Jovanovich, 1976.

Wolf, Michelle A., and Al Kielwasser, eds. *Gay People, Sex and the Media*. Binghamton, New York: The Haworth Press, 1991.

Worcester, David. *The Art of Satire*. Cambridge, MA: Harvard University Press, 1940.
Ziv, Avner. *Personality and Sense of Humor*. New York: Springer, 1984.
———. *National Styles of Humor*. New York: Greenwood Press, 1988.
———, ed. "Introduction." *Humor*, vol. 4, no. 2 (1991).
Ziv, Avner, and Orit Dadish. "The Disinhibiting Effects of Humor: Aggressive and Affective Responses." *Humor*, vol. 3, no. 3 (1990).

Name Index

Abrahams, Roger, 172
Abrams, M.H., 171
Adams, J., 171
Addams, Charles, 140
Allen, Melanie, 21, 173
Allen, Mitch, vii
Allen, S., 171
Allen, Woody, 47, 48, 57, 59, 60, 73, 76, 171
Allport, Gordon W., 172
Alter, Robert, 171
Anderson, Sherwood, 157, 171
Anton, 140
Apte, Mahadav, 1, 168, 169, 170, 171
Aristophanes, 55, 83, 86, 88
Aristotle, vii, 37, 38, 47, 48, 51, 105
Ashbee, C.R., 171
Attardo, Salvatore, 66, 76, 171
Ausubel, Nathan, 171

Bachem, Paul, 149, 152
Bakhtin, Mikhail, vii, 75, 76, 79, 80, 88, 103, 159, 160, 170, 171
Bateson, Gregory, 26, 27, 106, 129
Becker, Stephen, 171
Bennett, D.J., 171
Benson, Thomas W., 52, 60, 174
Bentham, Jeremy, 83
Berger, Arthur Asa, 117, 153, 155, 170, 171
Bergler, Edmund, 171
Bergson, Henri, vii, 28, 41, 42, 43, 44, 48, 66, 87, 105
Berlyne, D.E., 129
Bettelheim, Bruno, 171
Blair, Walter, 171
Boatright, Moady, 172
Bonaparte, Napoleon, 122, 123
Boskin, J., 172

Botkin, B.A., 172
Bouissac, Paul, 71, 72, 76
Brewer, John, 10, 19, 172
Brody, M., 172
Burke, Kenneth, 82, 83, 88, 172
Bush, Barbara, 149
Bush, George, 149
Butler, Samuel, 46, 48, 59, 60

Caen, Herb, 100
Cameron, William Bruce, 172
Campbell, Robert Jean, 13, 19, 173
Camus, Albert, 47
Cantril, Hadley, 172
Capp, Al, 172
Carroll, Lewis, 35
Cathcart, Robert, 101
Chabanne, Jean-Charles, 66, 76, 171
Chapman, Tony, 3, 4, 9, 19, 45, 48, 95, 101, 172
Charney, Maurice, 172
Clay, Andrew Dice, 57
Conrad, Paul, 144
Cousins, Norman, 172
Crumb, Robert, 141

Dana, Bill, 174
Davies, Christie, vii, 93, 94, 172
Dayan, Daniel, vii
Dionysius, 77
Douglas, Mary, ix, vii, 63, 108, 109, 116, 118, 172
Duncan, H. D., 172
Dundes, Alan, 172

Eco, Umberto, vii, 5, 6, 19, 172
Ehrenberg, Victor, 86, 88, 172
Elliot, Bob, 73, 76, 172
Ellis, Richard, 92, 101, 118, 174

Subject Index

Joke and Humorous Text Index